Information Unlimited
The applications and implications of information technology

CW00822957

SMALL COMPUTER SERIES

Consulting editors **Jan Wilmink**
University of Twente

Max Bramer
Open University

Information Unlimited
The applications and implications of information technology

Ian Sommerville

Addison-Wesley Publishing Company

London • Reading, Massachusetts • Menlo Park, California • Amsterdam
Don Mills, Ontario • Manilla • Singapore • Sydney • Tokyo

Set by the author in Bookface Academic using NROFF, the
UNIX text processing system, at the University of Strathclyde,
Glasgow

Cover design by Design Expo Limited

Printed in Finland by OTAVA. Member of Finnprint.

British Library Cataloguing in Publication Data

Sommerville, Ian
   Information unlimited.–(Small computer series)
   1.   Technology–Information services
   I. Title   II. Series
   607   T10.5

   ISBN 0-201-14636-3

Library of Congress Cataloging in Publication Data

Sommerville, Ian.
   Information unlimited.
   (Small computer series)
   Bibliography: p.
   Includes index.
   1. Microcomputers.   2. Microprocessors.
3. Microelectronics.   4. Electronic data processing–
Social aspects.   I. Title.   II. Series.
QA76.5.S6536   1983   303.4'834   83-3757

ISBN 0-201-14636-3 (pbk.)

ABCDEF   89876543

Contents

Preface

The introduction of new semiconductor technology for building computers and other electronic equipment has meant a dramatic fall in the cost of computers. They can now be applied in almost all areas of work and leisure and their introduction seems set to promote social and economic changes which are as profound as those seen during the Industrial Revolution of the 19th century. There have been countless radio and television documentaries and newspaper articles about this new technology and its effects on society. This media exposure has resulted in the creation of an associated 'new mythology'. This mythology suggests that computers are all-powerful machines which can take over from man. Depending on the prejudices of the commentator, this means that computer technology will either save or destroy the world.

This book is an attempt to present a more balanced view of computers and related aspects of information technology. Information technology is the term which has been coined to describe machines which are used in the processing and communication of information. As well as computers, information technology embraces communications systems such as television and telephones. In future, computers and communications systems will be very closely linked and it will not really be possible to discern where the computer system stops and the communication system begins.

The book is aimed at readers from any background who are interested in computers and computing. It's written in non-technical language and you don't need background knowledge of maths or electronics to understand the topics covered here. I hope it will appeal to hobbyists who are looking for a book which gives them a broad perspective of information technology, to school, college and university students taking introductory courses in the subject and to anyone else who wants to know more about this vitally important topic.

This is neither a technical book discussing the workings of computers nor is it just a catalogue of future applications of information technology. Rather, selected application areas are looked at in some detail and existing computer uses in these areas are described. Possible future developments in these areas are suggested and I speculate on how these developments will affect society of the future.

As well as being interested in what computers and associated communication systems can actually be used for, I assume that the reader of this book has some interest in how these systems actually work. Therefore, wherever it is possible to explain, in simple terms, how a system works I have done so. Inevitably, however, this is not possible for all the applications which are described here. Not only would it make the book far too long, but the way in which some system work cannot really be understood without a lot of background knowledge of computers.

Unfortunately, in a new and expanding topic like information technology, it is impossible to avoid using some jargon and technical terms simply because there is no simple English equivalent of these terms. I have tried to minimise the use of jargon and where technical terms have to be used, they are defined in a glossary. Terms in the text which are emboldened like this – minicomputer – are all defined in the glossary.

There are 8 chapters in the book, each dealing with a separate topic. The first chapter is a bit technical and discusses the history of computers, how silicon chips are made and some aspects of communications technology. Although the information here is useful for helping the reader understand the remainder of the book, it is not entirely essential. The chapter may be skipped by readers who either know about such technicalities or who aren't interested in them at all.

Chapters 2 through to 6 discuss various aspects and applications of information technology. Chapter 2 looks at the nature of information itself and at systems for handling very large amounts of information. Chapter 3 considers everyday applications of computers in the home and in education and Chapter 4 looks at applications of computers in the office and in the factory. Chapter 5 discusses information technology and money and Chapter 6 describes how computers are coming to play an important role in medicine.

Chapter 7 moves away from immediate applications and discusses artificial intelligence which promises important new developments in future. These developments include computers which can see and talk and which can, to some extent, understand speech.

Throughout the book, specific social implications of information technology are covered in the appropriate chapter. Privacy of information is covered in Chapter 2, computer crime in Chapter 4 and unemployment in Chapter 6. However, Chapter 8 is entirely devoted to a discussion of the long-term social implications of information technology. It presents various scenarios, both optimistic and pessimistic, of a computerised future.

A number of films have been made in conjunction with this book and these show some of the applications which are described here. They are available on film or videocassette and have been made for use in an elementary course in information technology. These are particularly useful to teachers giving courses in this topic and further details of these productions are available from Audio-visual Services, University of Strathclyde, Glasgow, Scotland.

Acknowledgements

More people than is possible to name have helped me write this book. Whilst making the films referred to above many people talked to me about their work. Without their contribution, it would have been impossible to write this book. The film crew at Strathclyde University must also be mentioned. They tolerated my sometimes eccentric demands with patience and good humour.

Several of my colleagues provided invaluable criticism of initial versions of the text. Thanks are due to John Mariani, Bob Welham, Richard Fryer, David Hutchison and Jon Malone, all of Strathclyde University. Particular mention must also be made of Ron Morrison of St Andrews University who gave me an outsiders viewpoint and useful and constructive criticism.

A number of organisations kindly provided the photographs illustrating this book. They were IBM UK Ltd. (Figs. 1.5, 4.4, 5.3), Digital Equipment Co. Ltd. (Fig. 1.6), Scottish Television Ltd. (Fig. 2.1), the US Army (Fig. 1.1), Ford Photographic Unit (Fig. 4.3), the British Robot Association (Fig. 4.4), The Royal Bank of Scotland Ltd. (Fig. 5.1), and the Southern General Hospital, Glasgow (Figs. 6.1, 6.2). I am very grateful to all of them for their help.

Ian Sommerville
May 1983

Chapter 1
Information technology

The development of mankind as the dominant species on earth has been punctuated by a number of very important landmarks. These include the development of speech, the invention of writing, the invention of printing, the development of the railway system and the invention of the telephone.

All of these have one thing in common - they facilitate the handling and communication of information. Speech allowed information to be communicated from person to person and writing for information to be permanently recorded. Printing allowed multiple copies of information to be made and the railway system allowed information to be widely and cheaply disseminated in the form of letters, newspapers, and periodicals. Finally, the telephone and associated developments in telecommunications such as radio and television allowed the instant transmission of information from place to place.

Now I believe that over the last 40 years there have been two further developments which history will show to be of equal importance to the invention of writing and printing. These developments are the invention of the **digital** **computer** and the invention of the microchip.

The invention of the computer marked a very important step forward in the development of information technology. The pre-computer inventions discussed above were purely passive devices for transmitting or recording information. They did not change that information in any way. By contrast, the computer is an active device which can be instructed to analyse and modify the information which it stores or communicates.

The comparison of computers and microchips with writing and printing is deliberate. Just as writing made new developments possible but restricted knowledge to an elite, so too did the invention of the computer. It allowed important new developments in information processing but the use of computers was restricted to relatively few rich organisations. Printing made written knowledge universally available and is comparable with the microchip - this invention makes computers as much a part of everyday life as printed information.

However, it is not just computers on their own which are important. Communication systems are also changing radically. The development of microchips has directly resulted in cost reductions in all kinds of electronic equipment, particularly equipment which is used in telecommunications systems. It has made developments in other fields such as space technology possible. This reduces the costs of placing communications satellites around the earth. Furthermore, in parallel with the development of microchips, new cable making techniques have been developed which use glass rather than copper as the signal transmission medium. In future, these cables will be cheaper than copper cables, and be capable of transmitting much more information.

Both computer technology and communications technology are on the brink of dramatic new advances. They are converging and becoming closely related. Computers are becoming integral parts of communication systems and many computer applications depend on computers communicating with each other. This new technology - an amalgam of computer technology and communication technology - is termed information technology.

Information technology encompasses computers, telephone systems and television systems. As the technology develops, the distinction between these systems will become more and more blurred. Both telephones and televisions will incorporate computers. It will be possible to display computer data on your television and to send it elsewhere via your telephone or TV cable. Just as the majority of homes now have a telephone and a television, in future they will have one or more computers in everyday use.

Information technology will impinge on all areas of life - in the home, at school, in stores, in the hospital, and at work. It will radically change society just as technological developments in the 19th century changed society from being predominantly agricultural to being predominantly industrial. Because of the vastly increased communications capability, there may be less need for industries and people to group together. The trend of population movement from the country to the city could reverse. We may have to adjust to a completely different society where computers take over many present-day jobs, cash is obsolete and computer systems are an integral part of virtually every activity.

This book is mostly concerned with present and future applications and implications of this new information technology rather than how the systems actually work. However, a brief introduction to the technicalities of the subject makes the following descriptions of applications more understandable and this chapter is devoted to these technicalities. The topics covered here include the development of computers and computer applications, the making of microchips, new communications technology and how computers communicate.

1.1   THE DEVELOPMENT OF COMPUTERS

There is widespread disagreement as to what exactly constitutes a computer and when the first computer was actually built. Some suggest that the abacus, which has been in use in China for thousands of years, was the world's first computer. Others contend that a calculating machine invented in the 18th century by Blaise Pascal, a French mathematician, was the first real computer and yet others that the computing engines invented by Charles Babbage last century were the first computers.

As far as present day computers are concerned, these arguments are unimportant because modern computers are based on a completely different principle from early calculating machines. The important distinction is that present day computers are electronic digital computers whereas the early 'computing engines' were based on mechanical cogwheels or, in the case of the abacus, completely manually operated.

The distinction is this. Pre-digital computers are based on the changing value of some quantity such as a voltage or the position of a cogwheel and their precision is limited by the precision of the measurement of this change of state. Digital computers, on the other hand, make use of **binary numbers**, sequences of 1s and 0s, which can simply be represented as a set of switches. Their accuracy is, in principle, unlimited – to obtain greater accuracy, we simply add more switches. The use of this binary representation is discussed later in this chapter.

A further distinction between early computing machines and present day computers is that the instructions which tell the machine how to carry out the computation (the **program**) were manually input one by one on early machines. Now, the instructions are held within the machine itself. Modern computers have inbuilt memories to hold instructions and data and the instructions are fetched and executed from there.

The fact that the information in digital computers is represented as patterns of switch settings and that changes to that information merely means resetting switches is very important. Although switches can be implemented mechanically (light switches, switches on power tools, etc.), they can also be implemented electronically. The details of how this is done are unimportant – what is important is that electronic switches have no moving parts and can change state very quickly indeed.

This means that electronic digital computers are inherently much more reliable and very much faster than machines based on mechanical technology. There is, therefore, only a very tenuous relationship between mechanical 'computing engines' and modern electronic computers.

The first electronic digital computers were built in the late 1940s in the UK and in the USA although the idea of using electronic components to build a computer was probably put forward in Germany in the 1930s. The first practical, working electronic computer was called ENIAC and it was built at the University of Pennsylvania.

ENIAC was physically enormous - it occupied over 1800 square feet (about 200 square metres), weighed over 30 tons (30 000 kg), used 18 000 valves, 70 000 resistors and 10 000 capacitors. The machine needed a small power station to supply it and cost about half a million dollars to build. A photograph of this machine is shown in Figure 1.1.

EOSAC

The first experimental stored program computer, that is, the first computer where the program was held in the computer memory, was built at Manchester University in 1948 and the first practical stored program machine at Cambridge University in 1949. These were also large, expensive machines which consumed lots of power.

Fig. 1.1   ENIAC - the first electronic digital computer

The reason why these early computers were so large and expensive was that the switches making up the computer were implemented as thermionic valves. Thermionic valves look something like small complicated lightbulbs with filaments built into a glass envelope. They heat up in use and consume a relatively large amount of power.

If we still had to use valves to build computers, some early predictions which were made about the limited usefulness of computers would certainly have been true. However, in 1948, two American scientists invented a component which was to make valves obsolete and which, ultimately, was to lead to today's microchip. This component was the transistor.

Compared to valves, even the very first transistors were tiny, occupying only about a hundredth of the space taken up by a valve. Nowadays transistors have been micro-miniaturised to an incredible extent. Not only are they physically very much smaller than valves, they also need only a fraction of the power and the smaller the transistor, the less power it uses.

Transistors are made out of rather odd material called semiconductor, of which silicon is the best known example. The electrical properties of semiconductors are somewhere between those of electrical conductors like copper and insulators like polythene. What this means in practice is that semiconductors can sometimes act like a conductor and sometimes like an insulator. The actual electrical behaviour of a semiconductor can be modified by adding tiny amounts of impurities, typically boron or phosphorus and this gives the transistor manufacturer very precise control over the behaviour of particular types of transistor.

Very simplistically, transistors are like a sandwich with the filling being created by treating the semiconductor with a different impurity from the rest of the material. The effect of this is to create three regions in the transistor with the 'filling' electrically charged in the opposite way to the 'bread'. This is shown in Figure 1.2 which shows a transistor with positively charged 'bread' and negatively charged 'filling'.

If a positive voltage is applied at point C in Figure 1.2, this blocks the flow of current from A to B as the positive charges are repelled by the filling. If however, a negative charge is applied to C, positive charges are attracted from A and negative charges flow from the filling to B. Thus a current can flow. We can, therefore, turn the transistor on and off like a switch by changing the voltage at C. This can be done extremely quickly - in principle a transistor can be switched from one state to another hundreds of billions of times per second.

6

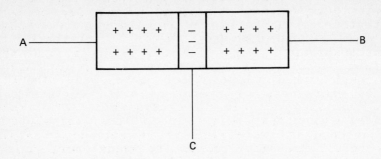

Fig. 1.2   A transistor

We shall come back to transistors later when we look at how microchips are made but now let us look at the effect of the invention of the transistors on the development of computers.

The transistor made valve-based computers instantly obsolete and by the early 1950s, the first commercial transistorised computers were available. From then on, the size of transistors and hence computers has been rapidly reducing along with their costs and their power requirements. This has meant that computers have steadily become smaller, cooler and cheaper and hence usable for many more applications than could possibly have been anticipated when valve machines were first built.

When the commercial possibilities of computers were recognised, the prime force of their development moved from research laboratories to commercial concerns. Further developments went hand-in-hand with the development of computer applications and this is discussed in the following section.

1.1.1 The development of computer applications

Like almost all initial applications of high-technology nowadays, the first applications of computers were military. ENIAC was used principally for ballistics computations and other early computers were used for navy navigational calculations and in nuclear physics.

The use of computers for numeric calculations was the sole application of these machines until 1951 when LEO, the first commercial computer went into operation. LEO, standing for Lyons Electronic Office, was built for a company who ran a chain of tea shops and was used for applications as diverse as computing payrolls and calculating optimal tea mixes. Lyons estimated that LEO could compute an employee's wages in 1.5 seconds compared to the 8 minutes taken when the wages were worked out manually by a clerk.

Throughout the 1950s, applications of computers in solving numerical problems remained dominant. A computer became increasingly essential for scientific institutions such as universities and research laboratories. However, commercial applications of computers were becoming more and more important and by the late 1950s, there were machines available which had been specifically designed for commercial computations such as payroll, stock control, etc.

In 1963, the real changeover from numeric applications to commercial applications came about when IBM launched its so-called third-generation computer. These were the first computers where more than one component was fabricated out of a single chunk of semiconductor and were larger, cheaper and faster than any machines available up till then. With the advent of this new series of computers, commercial computer applications took off. Computers became an integral part of the organisation of large companies looking after accounting, scheduling, stock control and all sorts of clerical tasks. The main application of computers became **data processing** rather than numeric calculation and data processing now accounts for about 90% of the present day applications of **mainframe** computers , that is, of large and powerful computer systems.

Around about the same time as the IBM third generation computer was introduced, another equally important development took place. This was the introduction of the **minicomputer** which was a physically smaller machine. Although minicomputers were slower than mainframe machines they were also much cheaper. The cheapness and size of the minicomputer meant that it became possible to include a computer as a component in other systems such as aircraft, ships, steel mills or chemical plants. The computer acted as a controller, watching over other system components and initiating actions on input from sensors.

The ability to incorporate a computer within some other system was increased in the 1970s with the development of the **microprocessor**. A microprocessor is an even smaller, cheaper computer which is about the size of a finger nail. This means that a computer, in the form of a microprocessor, can be incorporated in all sorts of fairly small machines and can act as a machine controller. Numerically, there are now probably more computers involved in control applications of one form or another than in any other applications. Computers are built into systems as diverse as children's toys and supersonic aircraft. As awareness of microprocessor technology grows, the use of computerised control will become almost universal.

1.2   THE MAKING OF MICROCHIPS

As I have said, I believe that the invention of the microchip is comparable with the invention of printing in importance. Unlike printing, however, the making of microchips cannot be undertaken with relatively simple equipment. It is an extremely complex process which relies on expensive, technically advanced fabrication technology.

First of all, let me define what I mean by the term 'microchip' which has been used fairly loosely up till now. A microchip is a small chip of semiconductor material on which are fabricated a number of electronic components such as resistors, capacitors and transistors. Microchips need not necessarily be computers - most electronic devices can be made in this way and a microprocessor is simply an example of a computer processing unit on a single semiconductor chip.

There are, literally, hundreds of different kinds of microchip ranging from fast and very complex microprocessors to relatively simple chips which are used in watches or remote control devices to switch TV channels. The technology underlying all these devices is the same. Because this technology allows electronic devices to be mass produced, almost all electronic equipment (not just computers) has become smaller and cheaper.

The technology used to make microchips is called very large scale integration which is usually shortened to VLSI . VLSI means that thousands of electronic components may be incorporated on a semiconductor chip and is itself the product of advanced technologies in physics, chemistry, electronics, and computer science.

The fundamental principle on which VLSI is based is that the operation of a transistor is virtually independent of the size of the transistor itself. Remember that a transistor is like a sandwich with the filling controlling whether the switch is on or off. As long as this fundamental configuration is maintained, it doesn't matter whether the size of this sandwich is half an inch, a tenth of an inch or a hundred thousandth of an inch.

The key to VLSI, then, is to build equipment which can take a circuit, designed by an engineer, and reduce it so that it can be directly integrated onto semiconductor material. There are really two stages to this process. First of all, a circuit design must be represented in such a way that it can be fabricated from a single chunk of material rather than as wires and discrete components. This process can only be carried out with the help of a computer and is far too complex to be described in simple terms here. The second stage is to take this representation and convert it to an actual silicon chip.

The mechanism which is used to create microchips is to build them up in layers. Remember that the electrical characteristics of semiconductors can be altered by introducing tiny amounts of impurities, so that by controlling this process, semiconductor devices can be built. Therefore, if somehow a layer of impurity-treated semiconductor is introduced into a pure section of the material everywhere that transistors are needed, a complete circuit can be built up.

The way in which these layers are built up is controlled by a mask which overlays the underlying semiconductor surface. The mask has gaps in it, setting out the relationship of the electronic components on the finished chip. The first part of the VLSI process, therefore, consists of translating a circuit design to a set of masks, one for each layer in the finished microchip.

Several individual masks are needed for each circuit, each defining the layout of one layer in the finished microchip. The conversion process from circuit design to a set of masks is so complex that it is impossible to carry it out manually. It requires the use of a computer-aided design system to calculate and draw the mask patterns which will implement the circuit in silicon.

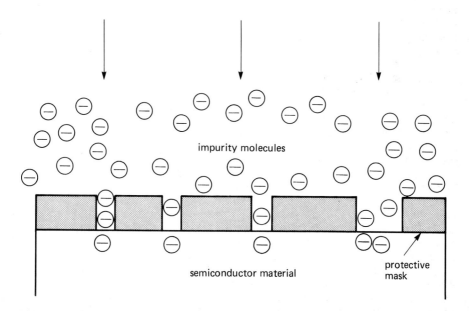

impurity molecules

semiconductor material

protective mask

Fig. 1.3   Introducing impurities into semiconductor

Say it is intended to make an array of transistors where each transistor is like that in Figure 1.2. One way of doing this is to take a layer of positive type material and introduce negative type 'filling' where we want the transistors to be. This 'filling' can be introduced by firing molecules of negative type impurity at the semiconductor, protecting the surface where we do not want impurity introduced. This is shown in Figure 1.3.

The semiconductor surface is protected by a mask which has gaps only where the impurity molecules may enter. The introduction of these impurities takes place in a chamber where a high pressure atmosphere of impurities is maintained. Because of the high pressure, these gradually work their way into into the semiconductor surface.

Using a similar process but at somewhat lower pressures, it is possible to ensure that the bombarding molecules do not actually penetrate the semiconductor surface but form a layer on top of the material. This way, layers of materials can be built up, some made by diffusion into the semiconductor surface and others made by deposition on the surface.

The first set of masks for a particular circuit are about 24 inches (60cm) square whereas the final chip is perhaps a quarter of an inch (8mm) square. The reduction from initial mask to final chip is made in two stages. Firstly, the mask itself is photographically reduced to create a new mask which is about 10 times the size of the final microchip. Secondly, a projection process, as shown in Figure 1.4 reduces the mask image to the ultimate chip size.

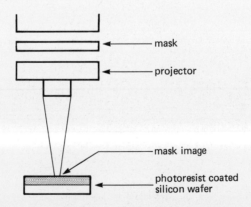

mask

projector

mask image

photoresist coated
silicon wafer

Fig. 1.4   Projecting mask onto semiconductor

The microchips themselves are not made singly but in an array on a circular wafer of semiconductor material (usually silicon). This wafer is cut from a single crystal of silicon grown under strictly controlled conditions so that it is ultra-pure. The wafer is roughly 10cm in diameter and is is about the thickness of a piece of paper. Up to several hundred chips may be made on a single silicon wafer.

Before the mask is projected onto the wafer, the silicon is coated with a material called photoresist which hardens on exposure to light. Those areas of the photoresist which correspond with clear areas on the circuit mask harden, thus producing a negative of the mask on the silicon wafer. During this projection, many copies of the mask are made on each wafer - stepping motors move the wafer along and across the projection field to create each mask copy.

As the photoresist which has not been exposed to light remains soft, it can be removed by using photographic chemicals called developers. The next stage in the process, then, is to develop away the unexposed photoresist. This leaves gaps in the photoresist covering the wafer. Impurities can penetrate the semiconductor surface through these gaps. The impurity bombardment then takes place as shown in Figure 1.3. The final stage makes use of acid to etch away the remaining photoresist leaving the silicon-impurity layer on the wafer.

This process of coat, expose, develop, bombard, etch is repeated for each distinct layer which is to be created in the silicon. Simple microchips may have only four or five different layers whereas the most complex microprocessor chips can have up to eleven distinct layers created.

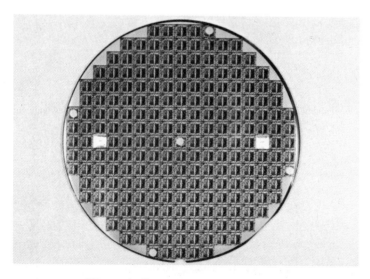

Fig. 1.5   Finished wafer

In all cases, the very last layer is a metallic layer which lies on the chip surface and makes electrical contacts between the different chip components. A photograph of a finished wafer made up of several hundred chips is shown in Figure 1.5.

Because the size of the components in a microchip is so small, a tiny error in the manufacturing process, a slight flaw in the silicon wafer, or even a speck of dust can ruin a microchip. Not only does this mean that chip fabrication must be carried out in ultra-clean surroundings, it also means that each and every chip must be tested to ensure that it works.

The first stage of testing takes place on the wafer itself immediately after the fabrication process. A computer-controlled testing machine uses a set of very fine probes to pass a small current through the chip. This checks that the chip actually behaves as a circuit and that components and connections are not misformed. Wafers which have more than a given number of defective chips are scrapped.

After this initial test, those chips which have passed the test are separated from the wafer using a cutting machine equipped with a very fine, diamond-toothed saw. They are then mounted in holders and electrical connections made between contacts on the chip and the pins on the holder. They then undergo further testing to check that no faults have been introduced in the cutting and mounting stages. A photograph of finished chips, mounted in holders, is shown in Figure 1.6.

Fig. 1.6   Finished microchips

It is a very expensive business to set up in microchip manufacturing. It requires expensive and complex optical, chemical and electronic equipment as well as many highly skilled technicians. However, once set up, microchips of different kinds can be made in their thousands and the unit cost of each chip is very low indeed. Simple chips may cost as little as a few pence and even complex microprocessor chips only cost a few pounds or dollars.

As an illustration of how the process of VLSI has changed computing, recall that the first computer, ENIAC, weighed over 30 tons, occupied over 1800 square feet and cost around half a million dollars to build. A modern microcomputer of equivalent power made up of a number of microchips costs less than 200 dollars, weighs about 3lbs and takes up the same amount of space as a pile of two or three paperback books. Furthermore, it is infinitely more reliable than ENIAC and very much easier to use.

1.3   TELECOMMUNICATION TECHNOLOGY

So far, this chapter has concentrated on computer technology without saying a great deal about complementary aspects of information technology concerned with new telecommunication systems. Just as VLSI is in the process of revolutionising computer systems, new technical developments are radically increasing the capabilities of communications systems. These new developments mean that there will be important changes in telecommunications in the very near future.

You don't need to know how computers work to understand the material in this book, nor do you need to understand the workings of telephone and television systems. In this section, therefore, I shall concentrate on new developments in communications technology such as fibre optics, cable television, and satellite communications rather than describing how communications equipment actually works. Taken together, these new developments will affect virtually everyone in the world and will vastly improve personal telecommunication facilities almost everywhere.

1.3.1 Fibre optics
At the time of writing, virtually all cables which are used for telecommunications are made out of copper. The reason for this is due to the molecular structure of that metal which makes it the most suitable material for transmitting communication signals. However, these copper cables do have two major disadvantages:

(1)   The amount of information which can be carried on a copper cable is limited by the thickness and

the construction of the cable. For example, thin copper cable such as that used in telephones cannot carry television signals or large amounts of computer data. To carry such signals requires the use of co-axial cable which is expensive to manufacture and even this type of cable has limited signal capacity.

(2)   The world supply of copper is limited. As this metal is also the principal constituent of electrical power cables, there is increasing demand for a limited supply of this material. Inevitably, this means that the price of copper cable is steadily increasing as demand starts to outstrip supply.

Fortunately, new developments in cable technology have now come to fruition and an alternative cable material is now available. That material is glass. In it familiar uses, windows, glasses, jugs, test tubes, etc., glass is a brittle substance which seems to be quite unsuitable as a material for making cable. However, when molten glass is spun into fibres about the thickness of a human hair, it becomes flexible and strong. Such cables are called fibre optic cables.
By using glass to make cables, the disadvantages associated with copper cables are avoided:

(1)   The main ingredient in glass making is silica sand which lies around the seashore in more or less unlimited quantities. Even the expense of mining is avoided - the sand can be collected with earthmoving equipment. The cost of fibre optic cables, therefore, is not highly dependent on raw material costs.

(2)   Simple single strand fibre optic cable can carry more information than even co-axial copper cable. In fact, a fibre optic cable made up of glass fibres about the thickness of a hair can carry tens if not hundreds of TV channels at the same time.

Fibre optic cables transmit signals in the form of light rays produced by a laser. They depend for their operation on a physical phenomenon known as total internal reflection which means that once a beam of light is introduced into the cable it bounces off the sides rather than diffusing out as if the cable was like a window. The direction of signal transmission, therefore, is always along the length of the cable.
As existing systems are rewired with fibre optic cable and new systems are introduced, there will be a dramatic increase in communications capability. The interchange of large amounts of computer data or

television signals will be cheap and straightforward. In conjunction with satellite communications, discussed in the following section, this will result in greatly increased use of national and international telecommunication systems.

1.3.2 Communications satellites

The idea of a geostationary communications satellite was first put forward by the science fiction writer Arthur C. Clarke as long ago as the 1940s. At the time, it was considered another figment of his fertile imagination but less than 20 years later, the first communications satellite (TELSTAR) was launched. Now such satellites are widely used for international communications. Within some large countries like India, there are proposals that some long-distance national communications should go by satellite.

A communication satellite works as follows. A satellite, equipped to receive and transmit signals, is positioned in a geostationary orbit above the equator. A geostationary orbit is about 23 500 miles high and is an orbit where the orbiting speed of the satellite is the same as the speed of rotation of the earth. Therefore, to an observer on earth, the satellite appears to be stationary. In fact, it is actually moving at the same speed as the spot on the earth where he or she is standing.

Communications signals do not actually bounce off the satellite in the same way as a light beam bounces off a mirror. Rather they are transmitted from a ground station to the satellite. They are received and then re-broadcast by a transmitter on the satellite to be picked up by a receiving station on earth.

Until recently, building and placing a satellite in orbit was very expensive so that communications satellites have only been used for military communications and for tariff paying telecommunications like international telephone calls and television transmissions bought by TV companies. However, the cost of these satellites is now falling for two reasons:

(1)   The general costs of electronic equipment is tumbling because of VLSI. This means that it is becoming much cheaper to build the communications satellite itself.

(2)   The cost of placing a satellite in orbit is falling because of developments in space technology. These include re-usable space vehicles such as the US space shuttle and low-cost booster rockets like the European Space Agency's Ariane rocket.

It is clear that if a satellite is positioned 23 500 miles above the earth, it can be seen from a large part of the earth. As broadcast TV depends on line of sight transmission where the receiving aerial is visible from the transmitter, satellite transmission of TV signals means that these signal can be received over a very wide area. With satellite broadcasting, the way is open for international television networks to supplement existing local and national TV stations.

However, satellite broadcasts do require a special type of aerial to pick them up. This aerial is shaped like a dish and is about a metre in diameter. Although it could readily be installed by individual domestic users, it is more likely that a central local aerial in each area will intercept the signals from the satellite and pipe them to individual users using a fibre optic cable. This is just one manifestation of cable television, a topic which is discussed in the next section.

As well as television signals, satellite communications will also be used to send computer data, facsimiles of printed information, and telephone conversations. It may soon be cheaper to place a satellite in orbit than to lay a long distance, high-capacity cable so even national communications could become satellite based particularly in large, sparsely populated countries such as Australia, Canada, and Brazil.

Furthermore, the capacities of these satellite communications will be such that it will be possible to increase significantly the number of personal communication systems at little extra cost. Home telephones, as well as being used for person to person voice communication, may also be able to exchange computer data and pictures. A telephone in the car, communicating directly with a satellite, will be available for those that want it and even personal hand-held communicators could be commonplace by the end of this century.

1.3.3 Cable television

In the following chapter, the possibility of people interacting with their television is discussed making television a two-way rather than a one-way communications medium. Such interaction is not really possible with broadcast television but is possible when TV signals are transmitted through a cable rather than broadcast through space. This section concentrates on the development of cable television. It explains how it is possible to transmit many television channels at the same time on the same cable and how interactive television, where the viewer interacts with the programme being broadcast, can be implemented.

Cable television is not new. It was originally developed to serve poor reception areas where an aerial was installed at the best reception point and the TV signal fed by cable to each individual household. A diagram of this is shown in Figure 1.7.

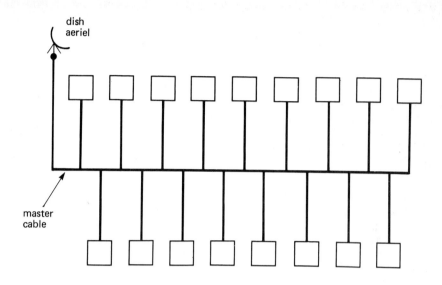

dish aeriel

master cable

households connected via branch cables

Fig. 1.7   Cable television

More recently, the same kind of system has been introduced in parts of the United States offering specialised programmes transmitted by cable to subscribers who pay specially for these particular programmes. These specialised programmes can be programmes on particular topics, news or sport or can be strictly local programmes where instead of the TV signal being received by a master aerial, it can be generated by a local TV station and fed directly into the cable network. There is no reason why dozens of TV channels cannot share the same cable with viewers only picking up those channels which they are willing to pay for.

To understand how it is possible to have signals transmitted at the same time along the same cable and, indeed, to understand how many different channels can be transmitted simultaneously, I must introduce the ideas of signal frequency and bandwidth.

Television signals, like radio waves, light, and X-rays are so-called electromagnetic waves which are transmitted at the speed of light. All kinds of waves obey a universal rule that their transmission speed is equal to the number of waves per second (the frequency)

18

multiplied by the length of the waves (the wavelength).

We can get an intuitive idea of this by considering waves made by a tap dripping into a bath of water. The faster the drip (the frequency), the closer together are the waves (the wavelength). If we slow down the drip speed, the waves become further apart so that the product of frequency and wavelength is always the same.

The range of frequencies of electromagnetic waves is very wide indeed ranging from ultra-low frequencies of a few waves per second to billions of waves per second. Television signals normally occupy only a small part of this frequency spectrum around about a hundred million waves per second.

However, the range of frequencies of television signal transmission is much greater than the frequency range needed to encode and transmit any one TV channel. It's not worth going into details of how pictures and sound are encoded for transmission - its sufficient to know than each channel only needs a fairly small frequency band to carry its information. The term bandwidth is used to describe the frequency range which can be transmitted on a cable or any other signal transmission medium.

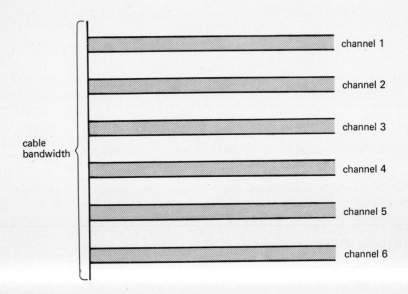

Fig. 1.8   Frequency allocation on a cable

Fibre optic cables and even co-axial cables can actually carry a wide range of frequencies so that many channels can be transmitted on the same cable. All that is needed is to encode these signals so that they don't interfere with each other. This encoding involves shifting the frequencies of each channel so that they each take up a small part of the cable's frequency range. This is illustrated in Figure 1.8.

The television set must contain a decoder which can be tuned to pick out a particular frequency range and convert this to a form which can be displayed on the screen. All televisions are equipped with such a decoder, designed to operate over the range of frequencies used by broadcast television. Exactly the same kind of system is used to decode signals received from a cable.

It is a straightforward matter to limit programmes on a cable to those who have paid for them. Viewers don't actually pay for programmes as they are transmitted but rent a decoder which is necessary for picking up these particular programmes. Without the decoder, the viewer who attempts to tune in to signals which have not been paid for will not be able to pick up pictures or sound from these signals.

Given a cable, it is relatively simple to implement two-way interactive television. Input signals occupy the major part of the bandwidth of a cable but a range of frequencies may be reserved for viewers responses. Any response from the viewer is transmitted on this frequency band.

This is only one of the numerous implications of transmitting TV on a cable rather than broadcasting it and conversion to cable based systems is likely to radically change television as we know it. These implications and changes are described in Chapter 2.

1.4   COMPUTERS AND COMMUNICATIONS

New communications systems such as satellites and fibre optics will result in vastly increased television services but, equally importantly, they will reduce the costs of data communications. This will allow world-wide networks of computer systems to be set up. This section looks at some of the technical aspects of computer communications. In particular, we shall see how information can be encoded for communication and how the quality of the communication line affects the speed of signal transmission.

Until recently, the great majority of computer applications involved some kind of centralised computer system. The work to be done was brought to the same building as the computer, input to the machine and the output physically taken back to the computer users. All the data needed by the system and all of its input and output devices were held in one place.

Now this situation is changing. Computing resources are being distributed and information is transmitted to and from the computer via communication lines. One reason for the centralisation of resources was that computers were expensive and it made sense to bring all work to the machine so that it didn't spend long periods doing nothing. With the advent of cheap computers, however, it is cheaper to have a computer doing nothing than to spend time physically moving input and output from place to place - its better to take the computer to the work rather than bring the work to the computer.

Centralisation did have the advantage that it made the sharing of data and programs between different users fairly straightforward. Say the maintenance department of an organisation kept a record of equipment faults which it had to repair and the time spent on repairing each fault. The design department of the same organisation could make use of this information to pinpoint design flaws and improve the product design so that it became both more reliable and more easily maintained.

Distributing computers to where they are actually used makes this information sharing more difficult. Although it would be possible to physically carry the information, on a tape cassette say, from one computer to another, a better solution is to connect the computers together on a communications network. When information on one machine is required by another computer, it can be directly transmitted from machine to machine.

Fortunately, the communications network for computer communications already exists. The telephone network, although not ideal, can be used to transfer information from computer to computer. Therefore, there is no need for massive capital investment in communication lines before computer communications can be established.

Linking computers with communication lines opens up lots of new applications which single computers, on their own, can't handle. In the same way as solving some problems requires groups of people to communicate with each other, some problems to be solved by computer require cooperating machines. Indeed, information technology is really the technology of communicating computers and most of the applications covered in the rest of the book involve both computers and communication systems.

1.4.1 Binary coding of information

The system of number representation which is universally used by humans is the result of evolution rather than numeric convenience. Our system is based on the number 10. There are 10 digits and counting proceeds in powers of 10 - tens, hundreds, thousands, etc. Clearly this is a direct result of the fact that we have ten fingers and these formed the very first computing machine.

The number system we use is based on what is

sometimes called place notation. We count up to 9 then 'remember' the number of tens by putting a 1 to the left of the units digit. We continue to record the number of tens until we get to a hundred, then record the number of hundreds, and so on. This system of counting can be used with any number system - it doesn't have to be based on 10. For example, a system based on the number 12 would actually be more convenient than the one which we use at the moment as 12 has 4 factors whereas 10 has only 2. With a system based on 12, we would count up to 11, then record the number of 12s, count up to 11 12s + 11 then record the number of 144s and so on.

Computers make use of a number system based on 2 called the binary system. With this system, we count up to 1 then record the number of 2s, count up to 3, then the number of 4s, etc. Because the number of digits needed to record a number in any system is the same as the base of the system, the binary system needs only 2 digits, 0 and 1.

As far as people are concerned, binary numbers are not very convenient to work with. The reason for this is that the binary representation of most numbers is much longer than the corresponding decimal representation - for example 15 in binary is 1111, 102 is 1100110, and 1030 is 10000000110. However, computers don't care about tedious lengths of numbers and the advantage of binary numbers is that they can be represented by a set of switches - 'off' meaning 0 and 'on' meaning 1.

Therefore 1030 could be represented in a computer by the following switch pattern:

on-off-off-off-off-off-off-off-on-on-off

The binary system is ideal for representing and manipulating numbers in a computer. If you are interested in the details of how this is done, binary representation is described in most elementary computer science textbooks.

Although it is quite easy to see how numbers can be represented in a computer, most computing doesn't actually involve numerical calculations but involves working with characters. These might be names and addresses, details of personal tax, commands typed into a home computer, or whatever. How can these characters be represented as binary numbers?

The idea of coding information is well known. In order to code information, we take one form of the information and apply some process which turns it into another form which means the same thing. For example, we might say 'tac' for 'cat' and 'xof' for 'fox', etc. As long as we know how to decode the information it is easy to work out the meaning of any coded message.

The same principle is used for representing characters in a computer. There is an internationally agreed coding standard for each letter so that 'A' is 65, 'B' is 66, 'Z' is 90, 'a' is 97, 'm' is 109, '(' is 40, etc. Notice that a different code is needed for upper and lower case letters. Therefore, a message such as 'Mary had a little lamb' would be coded:

    77 97 114 121 32 104 97 100 32 97 32 108 105 116 116
    108 101 32 108 97 109 98

Space has its own code (32) and in the code above the spaces are simply used to make the coded letters easier to read. In binary, the first word of the coded message (Mary) is represented:

    1001101 1100001 1110010 1111001

It is very tedious for us to deal with these codes but computers can handle them with ease. Character information, as well as numeric information, can therefore be easily represented and manipulated by computer.

1.4.2 Computer communications

The fundamental principle on which telecommunications equipment is based is that information can be encoded as some kind of varying electrical or electromagnetic signal which can be transmitted and decoded automatically. In a telephone, sound is converted to a varying electrical signal by a mechanism in the caller's telephone then converted back to sound in the listener's telephone. A television signal consists of picture and sound converted to an electromagnetic wave which is picked up by the viewer's aerial then converted, by the TV, back into sound and pictures.

For computers to communicate, therefore, there must be a way of representing computer data in binary form as a varying signal on a communication line. Fortunately, this is very easy indeed. Any binary number can be represented as a series of pulses on a line where a signal level of +1 represents the binary digit '1' and a signal level of -1 represents the binary digit '0'.

As an example of this, the 'pulse' representation of 'Mary' is shown in Figure 1.9.

Notice that there is no gap between the pulses of the individual letters in a word nor between the pulses representing individual binary digits. When computers agree to communicate they each start a timer and synchronise operations so that the sending computer sends a pulse every 1/10 000th of a second, say, and the receiving computer will expect to receive 10 000 pulses per second. If it finds that a signal is

maintained for 3/10 000ths of a second, it assumes that
this represents 3 pulses which are the same.

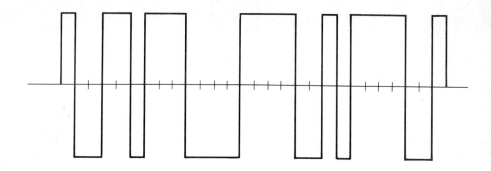

Fig. 1.9   Pulse representation of Mary

In all signal transmissions some information in the
original signal is inevitably lost because of
imperfections introduced by the transmission process.
A voice on a telephone sounds different from the same
voice in face-to-face conversation, a television
picture contains much less detail than the scene
originally filmed. The signal distortion introduced
during transmission is due to line interference called
noise. Noise is inherent in every signal transmission
medium and the amount of noise is related to both the
design of the communications line and the material used
in its construction.

The encoding of binary signals as +1 and −1 means
that the signal has some resilience to distortion on
the communications line. For example, say a +1 signal
was reduced to +0.7 and a −1 signal to −0.4. There is
still quite a difference between these signals so it
can be assumed that any positive signal is meant to be
'1' and any negative signal means '0'. This resilience
to distortion is very important as changing even a
single '1' to '0' could change the entire meaning of a
message.

The amount of noise which affects any particular
signal depends on the type of cable used for signal
transmission. Simple copper cables, like telephone
cables, are 'noisy' so can't be used for fast data
transmissions. However, fibre optic cables are not
inherently 'noisy' so thousands of characters per
second can be transmitted on these lines. Computers,
in future, will be connected by webs of glass fibre
with pulses of laser light flashing information from
machine to machine.

The mechanism of computer communication is easily
understood but before any communication can actually
take place, the computer systems involved must agree on

24

when to start and stop signal transmissions, what are
appropriate signal levels, etc.

As far as the actual signals on the line are
concerned, a device called a modem, attached to each
end of the communication line coordinates the computer
communication so that pulses on the line can actually
be translated to the correct binary numbers. Modems are
equipped with very accurate internal clocks so that the
operation of the sending and receiving modem can be
synchronised. The sender's modem translates the binary
pattern to pulses suitable for transmission on the
particular type of communication line being used and
transmits them to the receivers modem which turns them
back into a binary pattern for the receiving computer
to interpret. All the details of signal levels, etc.
are handled by the modems - the sending and receiving
machines need not take them into account.

At a higher level, the communicating machines must
agree on the format of messages, that is, they must
agree on what the transmitted signals actually mean.
This agreement is called a protocol. Protocols provide
information on when to start and stop transmission and
on the organisation of the transmitted information.
Because there are no universally agreed worldwide
standard protocols, one of the most difficult tasks
faced by the designer of a computer communications
network is the definition of protocols for inter-
computer communications.

1.5   SUMMARY

Information technology has resulted from a convergence
of computing technology and communications technology.
In future, more and more applications of computers will
be based on inter-computer communications. Computers
will be an integral part of virtually all
telecommunication systems. This chapter has introduced
some basic concepts of information technology.

The first part of the chapter concentrates on the
development of computing from the first, very
primitive, valve-based computers to today's
microcomputers. The first machines were really
scientific oddities and were so large and expensive
that their uses were very limited indeed. However, the
invention of the transistor in 1948 revolutionised
computer design and led directly to today's microchips.
Using smaller and smaller transistors, computers became
physically smaller, cheaper, and more powerful. The
early driving force in their development was probably
defence organisations but by the 1960s commercial
considerations became paramount. A computer is now an
essential tool in almost all commercial and
governmental organisations.

The ability of a transistor to act as a switch is

independent of the size of that device. Therefore, it is possible to actually build circuits out of chips of silicon where thousands of transistors are fabricated on a single chip. The second part of the chapter discusses the processes involved in making microchips. This is a very complex process requiring skills in electronics, chemistry, physics, and computer science. It revolves around photographically reducing circuits and building them up in layers on a silicon wafer.

Section 1.3 discusses new communications technologies. In the same way as the invention of the microchip is in the process of radically changing computing, these new technologies are changing telecommunications. Our present telecommunication system is limited by the capacity of the cables which are used. These do not allow the fast transmission of very large amounts of information. New techniques, however, using communications satellites and cables made of glass fibres mean that it will soon be possible to transfer vast amounts of information from place to place at relatively low cost. Probably the most important result of this will be the development of cable television. Not only will viewers have many many TV channels available, they will also be able to use their TV cables for computer communications.

The final section here discusses some of the mechanics of computer communications. It shows how computers can represent information in binary form. Not only is this a convenient way to represent information for processing, it can also be easily converted to pulses on a communication line. This section also discusses how noise on the line affects signal quality and how modems must be used to synchronise computer communications.

Chapter 2
Information unlimited

We live our everyday lives surrounded by a sea of information - from radio, television, books, newspapers, personal observations, etc. Normally, most of this information just washes over us without ever entering our memory. We only select particular items of interest to us from the vast amount of information which we come across in the course of day-to-day living. This chapter discusses information in general. It considers how computers can help control this information and make much more of it readily available to us.

Information can be thought of as 'the communication of knowledge' - how we actually get to know things about the world. An American mathematician called Shannon devised a mathematical definition of information which is very important to those actually involved in designing and building computer systems. This mathematical definition is unnecessarily complicated as far as understanding the material in this book is concerned so a less formal, more intuitive definition will be used.

It is very important to distinguish 'information' from the medium by which that information is actually carried. For example, you might learn to bake a cake by reading a recipe book, by talking with a friend, or by watching a demonstration of cake baking on television. The knowledge communicated - how to bake a cake - is quite independent of how you actually obtained that knowledge.

Furthermore, information is also quite distinct from its representation. A recipe for baking a cake might be written in French, English, Japanese, or any other language. For any particular language, the representation will only be understood by speakers of that language. Nevertheless, the information in the recipe - how to bake a cake - is exactly the same, in spite of the fact that it is represented differently in each language.

Information is therefore something which is quite independent of representation and medium. It is this fact that makes computers so useful in storing and processing information. We have already seen in

Chapter 1 how information (as characters) can be stored and transmitted in a computer where the information is represented as binary strings of ones and zeros. In principle at least, any information whatsoever - words, pictures, sounds, etc. - can be converted to binary form (the technical term is digitised) and stored in a computer.

One of the advantages of storing information on a computer is that the information may be stored in a very compact way. For example, using existing technology, approximately 50 copies of this book could be stored on a magnetic disk about the size of a long playing record. In a very few years, video disks will be used for storing computerised information. It will be possible to store over 10 000 books like this on a single video disk.

However, a more important advantage of using a computer to store information is that we have the option of using the computer to process the information in some way. This processing can take an almost infinite variety of forms. If the information is converted to a television picture, say, the computer could change all reds to blue and vice versa. It can take a US television picture made up of 525 lines and convert it to a UK picture made up of 625 lines. If the information stored can be represented as text - this book for instance - the computer can scan the text and retrieve every page that contains particular words such as 'video disk' or 'television picture'.

The rest of this chapter looks specifically at computer applications concerned with the storage and processing of large amounts of information. It also considers one of the most pressing problems which results from the computer's ability to store and process information. This is the problem of maintaining personal privacy. How can control be exerted over the use of computers in storing personal information so that an individual's right to privacy is preserved?

2.1   INTERACTIVE TELEVISION

The colour television set has become a facility which is available in more or less every home in the developed countries and, even in underdeveloped countries, television sets are common. Every country in the world has some kind of television service made up of news, documentary, and entertainment programmes.

Until very recently, television was technically limited to be a passive medium. Programmes were transmitted by electromagnetic signal, picked up by an aerial and displayed on the TV screen. The viewer had the option of accepting these programmes or switching the TV set off. He or she had no control over when to accept the programmes, no ability to select the particular type of programmes that he or she preferred, and no way in which he or she could repeat parts of programmes or news items of interest.

Some of these restrictions have been lifted by the advent of reasonably priced, microprocessor controlled video recorders. The low cost of microelectronic components has meant that these machines are now available on the consumer electronics market and many people have supplemented their TV set with a video recorder.

These video recorders allow television programmes to be stored and viewed at the convenience of the viewer. They enable parts of programmes to be repeated and action to be slowed down or speeded up. In general, they represent a significant move towards giving the viewer control over his or her television service.

However, video recording machines do not allow viewers to interact with their televisions. Indeed, whilst television signals are transmitted through space like radio waves, it is practically impossible for the viewer to interact with his or her television and communicate directly with the television service.

The ability to interact with the television can only come when programmes are transmitted along some kind of physical communication line rather than through space. Using the same cable and relatively simple electronic equipment, the viewer can send his own signal back to the source of the original television signal.

The idea of cable television has already been introduced in Chapter 1 and the details aren't repeated here. As well as improving reception, it offers the opportunity of providing many television channels to the viewer which might cover specialised topics, news and sport, or which might be strictly local programmes giving local news and information. Cable television has been available in parts of the USA since the late 1970s. Experience has been very mixed - some channels are very good, others are dreadful. The potential is there but, at the moment, there are not enough professional production units to provide high quality programmes on all of the available channels.

Once a household is connected to a cable TV network, it becomes possible to interact with the television programmes as they are actually being transmitted. In technical terms, this is called 'real-time' interaction. Viewers might be able to give their opinions on a politician's speech as it is being made, vote for the best shot in a football game or even take part in TV quiz games without leaving their armchair.

In Chapter 1, the idea of bandwidth was introduced and it was explained how a number of television channels could actually be transmitted simultaneously on the same cable. Each channel is allocated its own particular frequency range. A decoder in the set selects that channel's signal and converts it to a signal which can be displayed on the TV screen. Interactive television merely requires that the viewer's signals are allocated a frequency band which does not conflict with any of the television broadcast signals.

Interactive television depends on both the sender and the receiver of the signal being equipped with computers which control the communications on the television cable. Typically, each user connects a home computer to his or her television and types responses into that machine. The computer converts the response to the appropriate signal frequency for interaction and puts it into the cable. Normally, responses would be very short, say less than 10 characters, so they can be transmitted to the TV station in millionths of a second.

The television station is equipped with a large computer which constantly scans incoming signals looking for viewer's responses. These can always be recognised because no other signals are transmitted at that frequency. When a response is detected, the TV station computer converts that response back into the form originally typed by the user. The TV station's computer can react very quickly indeed so it can collect and collate responses from hundreds of different viewers.

Experimental interactive television stations are already in operation in parts of the United States but when simply used in conjunction with broadcast television they are really more of a gimmick than a particularly useful facility.

Interactive television systems require a slightly different network organisation from the so-called 'tree and branch' system shown in Figure 1.7. Rather than households being connected directly to a master cable, they are connected to a local minicomputer which is connected to the master cable. This minicomputer acts as a controller for the two-way communications traffic on the cable.

Interactive television systems will become much more useful when they can be connected to a computerised library of television productions. In the same way as books can be stored in a library and made generally available, so too can TV programmes. However, rather than being stored as tapes, the programmes can be electronically encoded and copied to the viewer's equipment when required. Only a single master copy of each programme need be held by the library.

When the viewer wishes to see a particular programme, he or she can use the library index to find the programme required then request the library computer to send that programme to his or her video recorder using the cable TV network. This transmission can be made at very high speed as there is no need for the viewer to see the programme as it is transmitted. When transmission is complete, the programme can then be replayed at the viewer's convenience.

This will mean vastly increased access to television productions. There are likely to be thousands of programmes on offer and the TV viewer need not be restricted by the schedules as to what and when he views.

2.2   TEXT AND TELEVISION

Television is normally thought of as a pictorial medium where information is transmitted as pictures with an accompanying sound track. However, there is no reason why those television pictures should not be made up of text so that the viewer can actually read information from the television screen.

This ability has already been used by some television companies in the provision of what are termed teletext systems. In the UK, there are two such systems, CEEFAX broadcast by the BBC and ORACLE run by the independent television companies.

Fig. 2.1   A teletext page

These teletext systems continually broadcast pages of information which may be received by sets fitted with the appropriate decoder. An example of a typical teletext page is shown in Figure 2.1.

Information pages are transmitted at a rate which is much faster than we can read. About 4 pages are transmitted every second. In order to read a page, therefore, it must be 'trapped' and 'remembered' by the TV set. When the viewer decides which page he wishes to read, he keys in that page number into a small hand-held controller. The TV set has a built-in teletext decoder system consisting of a microprocessor and an area of memory large enough to store one teletext page. When the page is transmitted, this decoder copies the page into its memory. Once the page has been copied, the computer displays it on the TV screen until the viewer requests some other page or switches off the teletext facility.

As far as the viewer is concerned, teletext pages and television programmes are broadcast simultaneously and he or she can switch, at will, from one to the other or even display teletext sub-titles at the same time as television programmes. In fact, the teletext system works by making use of 'gaps' in the television transmission and broadcasting the teletext pages during the 'gaps'. Of course, we don't see these gaps because they are very short indeed - much shorter than our eyes can possible notice. As a result, the television transmission appears to be continuous.

Existing teletext systems act as electronic newspapers providing news, weather, forecasts, entertainment guides, features, etc. They have the advantage over conventional newspapers that the system pages can be updated as news becomes available so that they always present the most up-to-date news to the reader.

Because of this, and because the dissemination of news on such systems is much cheaper than producing a newspaper, it has been suggested that, in future, printed newspapers will become obsolete. All news could be distributed as some form of teletext system.

This is very unlikely. Printed newspapers are, by their very nature, portable. They can be read anywhere - on a train, in a pub, whilst waiting for a dental appointment, etc. Reading a newspaper requires no special equipment or power supply and can be carried out without intruding upon anyone else. Teletext systems require a television which is inherently obtrusive, unportable, and which needs a power supply. With current television technology, it is inconceivable that teletext systems will replace newspapers.

Let us assume, however, that in future a portable, battery operated, flat screen, pocket sized television will be developed (this actually seems quite likely).

Might electronic newspapers then become viable? Again, I think, the answer is no. Teletext systems suffer from the inherent disadvantage that television screens are relatively low-resolution - that is - they cannot show really fine detail. For normal viewing, the resolution is adequate but it is actually impossible to generate small characters which are readable on a TV screen. This fact limits the page size in teletext systems to 24 lines of 40 characters - 960 characters in all.

As typical newspaper columns are about 25 characters wide, each teletext page therefore represents about 5 column inches (12.5 column centimetres). A typical newspaper page of 8 columns by 21 inches would therefore require about 33 teletext pages to provide the same amount of text. The reader would spend almost as long changing teletext pages as he or she did reading!

What then will be the role of broadcast teletext systems in future? At the moment, they are an interesting technical innovation mostly used for supplementing television news programmes. Whilst this application will continue, it seems unlikely that teletext systems will have any significant impact on the traditional newspaper market.

The role which is best suited to broadcast teletext is to back up television programmes with printed information. This might take a number of forms. For deaf viewers and for viewers of foreign language programmes, sub-titles might be provided; instructional programmes such as cookery demonstrations might be complemented by teletext recipes; educational programmes might have detailed background material made available on teletext.

The power of television as an educational medium can be vastly increased by teletext. Television is a 'what' rather than a 'how' medium. It can clearly show what a dam looks like, what a word processor can do, what happens when different chemicals are mixed. However, it is not well suited to describing the mathematics involved in designing a dam, how to program a word processor, or how to calculate chemical reaction details. Detailed information on how to do something is normally much better presented as text and it is for this purpose that broadcast teletext is most useful. This use of teletext in education is covered in more detail in Chapter 3.

2.3   VIDEOTEX

As well as broadcast teletext systems, teletext systems are also available which use the TV as a display unit and which pass information to the TV using an ordinary telephone line. These are normally distinguished from broadcast teletext systems by terming them **videotex** systems. Until recently, such systems were called **viewdata** systems but for some reason this name has been abolished in favour of the less descriptive term 'videotex'.

Private videotex systems have been developed by a number of large companies and public systems are also available in some parts of North America and western Europe. In the UK, the public system, run by British Telecom, is called Prestel and this will be described here as a typical example of videotex systems.

Prestel was the first public videotex system in the world and it offers users access to information on a wide variety of topics – stock exchange prices, travel information, weather reports, job opportunities, mail order lists, etc. Although the same display technology as broadcast teletext systems is used, Prestel differs from these systems in a number of respects:

(1)   Prestel information pages are not broadcast through space. Instead, users of Prestel must make a direct connection with the Prestel computer to access the information they require. This connection is made via an ordinary telephone line.

(2)   Prestel is not free – users must pay for information from the system.

(3)   Prestel pages are not output in sequence whilst the user waits for the required page to come along. Rather, the user keys in the number of the page that he wants. The Prestel computer selects this page from its memory and transmits it to the user's TV.

(4)   Prestel users can actually interact with the Prestel computer to order goods, make a theatre booking, cancel an airline reservation, etc.

The basis of Prestel and Prestel-like systems is a central computer with all information pages stored in its memory. This machine has many telephone connections available and the user dials the computer to make the connection. Once a connection is made, he or she can then interact with the computer using a small hand-held control unit to request pages for display.

Videotex is potentially much more useful than broadcast teletext systems because it provides access to hundreds of thousands of information pages and because of the fact that users can actually interact with the videotex computer.

As far as the user is concerned, he or she has

exclusive access to the videotex computer although, in practice, there are many people making use of the system at the same time. There are two factors which allow many users to make use of a videotex system at the same time:

(1)   Most of the time that people spend using a system like Prestel is spent reading information on a page. The user is not making any demands on the system computer. Whilst he or she is reading, the computer can service other users.

(2)   The computer controlling the videotex system can switch very quickly indeed from one user to another. In practice, the switching time may only be a few thousandths of a second so that many users can be serviced in the time that it takes to key in a request. The Prestel computer continually looks at all the telephone lines which are attached to it to see if any line has made a request for a page. If so, it processes that request, otherwise it simply moves on to look at another line. The scan through the lines and the request processing is so fast that all the lines can be examined in the time that it takes a single user to call for a page.

As a result of these factors, the user does not actually notice that he or she is sharing the computer with perhaps a hundred other people.

The biggest single advantage of videotex systems is that they are easy-to-use. They use familiar technology - the television and the telephone - and the user need not learn any special commands to make use of the system. Within five minutes of getting started, an absolute beginner can make effective use of these systems.

In this respect, videotex differs from most other computer based information retrieval systems. Most systems require special terminals and, to access information, the user must learn specialised instructions required by the system. Such requirements intimidate many users who are unfamiliar with computers and computing jargon with the result that they do not make effective use of the computer system.

Because of their ease of use, videotex systems are likely to become widely used in commerce and industry. They will supply information to all levels of staff without the need for extra training. Whilst smaller organisations will make use of public videotex, within large organisations private videotex systems will be available running on the firms own computer. These systems will be able to exchange information with each other and with public videotex and it may even be possible for information stored on private systems to be made publicly available through the videotex computer.

The pages in a videotex system such as Prestel are organised in a hierarchy in very much the same way as family tree charts are hierarchical. In fact, in computing terminology, the organisation of videotex pages is called a tree because it resembles an upside-down tree, with roots at the top and leaves at the bottom. An example of a hierarchical organisation, like that of Prestel, is shown in Figure 2.2. In this diagram, index pages are shown as circles, and information pages as rectangles.

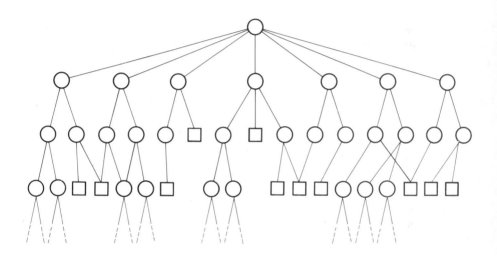

Fig. 2.2   Hierarchical Organisation of Videotex Pages

Notice that near the top of the tree, nearly all the pages are index pages. This must be expected. When there are hundreds of thousands of pages, there needs to be lots of indexes and sub-indexes to enable users to find the page which they require.

There are two possible ways of accessing a Prestel page. Either the user types the full six digit page number into his controller or, alternatively, he can work his way down the hierarchy of Prestel index pages.

Working down through a hierarchy of indexes involves firstly, looking at the page at the top of the tree. That page refers to other indexes and pages which are lower down in the hierarchy. As well as giving their full page number, the index also gives an abbreviated page number (one or two digits). Punching this abbreviated number moves the user's view to that page.

It is possible to provide abbreviated numbers because, as well as an absolute and unique page number, any page may also have a number relative to some index. To give an analogy, say you were asking directions. You might be told "the house you are looking for is number 27" (absolute address) or "its the 3rd house past the monkey puzzle tree" (address relative to the monkey puzzle tree). Both of these sets of directions get you to the same place in the same way as an absolute and relative page number get the same Prestel page.

This addressing system works well as long as the information which you require is grouped together in the hierarchy. It must lie around the same branch of the tree. This means that as you work through the Prestel indexes, you get closer and closer to the required information.

However, the hierarchical organisation is not so good if the pages which you wish to access are scattered all over the system on different branches of the tree. When this situation arises, you have to laboriously traverse each branch of the tree to find the information which you want.

Another problem with the existing version of Prestel is that it offers the user a very small personal memory space. The system can remember the last three pages referenced by a user. He can recall these pages by pressing a single key. However, if he wants to look at a page which was referenced more than 3 pages ago, he must either know its full page number or must start at the top of the index hierarchy to find that page.

This may not be considered much of a disadvantage but, in fact, there are many applications where Prestel could be very useful indeed and which are more awkward than they ought to be because of this limitation.

For example, some Prestel pages are provided by holiday tour operators giving details of holiday availability. For someone who wants to make a last minute decision on a holiday, it is very useful to compare what's on offer from each travel company. Because Prestel is computer based its information can be completely up to date and last minute bookings can be immediately incorporated. In practice however, should the Prestel user wish to compare to compare prices and availability of different holidays, he or she must access pages from maybe ten or twelve different companies on four or five different resorts. This is very inconvenient because these pages can't be simply recalled but must be called up by their full six digit page number.

A final problem with Prestel is due to the nature of the teletext system itself. Because the system is entirely character oriented, the only graphics which may be displayed are block graphics where pictures are made up of blocks of characters. This makes for very low resolution, stylised graphics. It isn't possible to display colour photographs or other high resolution images on Prestel.

It has been suggested that one important use of Prestel might be as a mail order catalogue where viewers can refer to the catalogue and directly order goods by keying in their credit card number (the system already knows their name and address). However, a feature of mail order catalogues is that they are illustrated with photographs of the goods on sale and until a 'Picture Prestel' is available, the systems use for mail order will be restricted to goods such as wines, cameras, etc. This restriction is not inherent to videotex systems - the Canadian 'Telidon' system can display much higher resolution graphics than Prestel but needs more expensive adaptors to use it with a domestic TV set.

So far, Prestel has not been as successful as its designers had anticipated. There seem to be a number of reasons for this:

(1)   Using Prestel is not particularly cheap. As well as normal telephone call costs, the Prestel user must pay an extra charge for looking at some system pages.

(2)   Television sets equipped with Prestel decoders are much more expensive to buy or rent than ordinary TV sets. Domestic users are disinclined to pay these costs as well as paying for the use of the system.

(3)   Although there is an enormous amount of information available on the system (more than 250 000 pages), it doesn't cover all fields and some information providers do not keep their information up to date. A few experiences of out of date information tends to discourage users from making further use of Prestel.

(4)   The inherent limitations of the system, described above, make it unsuitable for storing many kinds of information, particularly that which does not fall into a single, clearly defined, category. This means that many potential information providers cannot make effective use of Prestel.

In principle at least, all these difficulties are surmountable but, as with any notable innovation, a 'chicken and egg' situation exists. When motor cars first became available, people were disinclined to use them because of poor roads yet because there were few cars, there was no economic justification in improving the roads. Similarly with videotex. Because there are relatively few users, information providers do not see any economic justification for providing information in videotex form. However, without lots of relevant information it is difficult to attract significant numbers of new users to the system.

To be fair, British Telecom, the inventors and providers of Prestel, are well aware of the problems and are working hard to improve the system. Furthermore, the cost of Prestel decoders is likely to fall significantly in the very near future as the required circuitry is integrated onto a microchip.

In spite of all this, however, it is still difficult to see videotex being widely used domestically because of the communications costs involved. Whilst business and industry will make increasing use of such systems, they are not likely to have significant impact in the home unless special off-peak telephone rates are made available.

However, it is perfectly possible that phone charges for videotex users will be reduced. After all, the telephone network is under utilised outside business hours and it is better to have some return from this even if the charges are not, strictly, economic.

2.4   DATA BASE SYSTEMS

Prestel is a simple example of a class of computer systems based on what is often called a data base. A data base is simply an extremely large amount of information, stored on a computer, and organised in such a way that the information can be readily retrieved, processed and revised. In Prestel, the data base consists of all the system pages and the system organisation is hierarchical to allow relatively easy access to information.

We have already seen some of the disadvantages of this hierarchical organisation. Because of these, the information processing needs of many organisations cannot be met by a data base organised as a simple hierarchical set of pages.

There are many other possible data base organisations. These organisations usually provide much more sophisticated searching facilities than videotex systems. The user need not work his or her way through a hierarchy of pages but can go directly to the information which is required. Furthermore, the data base system records the relationships of different items of information so that all information in a particular class, say, may be processed at the same time.

There are probably well over a hundred books available on data base systems and it is quite inappropriate to go into details of these systems here. However, to give a general indication of how data base systems can be used, consider a very simple data base holding a library catalogue.

The information held in the data base about each book might be as follows:

(1)   The book number.

(2)   The class number.

(3)   The title.

(4)   The date of purchase.

(5)   The author.

(6)   The publisher.

(7)   The number of copies held.

This information is held in what is normally called a record. Each and every book in the catalogue has its own record. The data base consists of all these records and the data base system provides a means of access to individual records.

To provide easy access to information, the data base system must create a number of indexes. One index is the author index where, given an author, the data base system can find all the records of books written by that author. Another index might be a title index and, perhaps, an index based on the book number. Potentially, if there are some number, say n, items of information associated with a record (n=7 in the above example), there may exist n indexes, each based on a different information item.

Recall that to access a Prestel page (a page is just like a record) the user had to work through a hierarchy of indexes. With the library catalogue system, this is not necessary. The user can ask for all books written by a particular author, can ask for all books with the words 'information technology' on the title or can ask for all books purchased since 1980.

The system becomes really powerful when it can answer questions based on combinations of indexes and on the basis of incomplete information. Say you wanted to find out all books which have information technology in the title and which were purchased since 1980. You might pose the data base system a question as follows:

find books title=*information technology* & date 1980-TODAY

This is a typical example of how a query to a data base system might be formulated. It is written in a stylised way and uses keywords (underlined) to tell the system what to look for. The above command can be interpreted as follows:

find books - means look in the data base of book information and its associated indexes

title=*information technology* - means look at the title index and select all books which have a title containing the phrase 'information technology'. The symbol * is useful when we want to give the system incomplete information. The * symbol can be read as 'anything' so *science means anything followed by science. Therefore *information technology* means anything followed by 'information technology' followed by anything.

date 1980-TODAY instructs the system to make use of the date index to find all books purchased between 1980 and the date the query is made.

The symbol & connecting the title and the date requests means 'and' so that books which contain information technology in the title and which were purchased since 1980 are actually selected for display.

Such a system is more precise than a page-oriented system such as Prestel but requires that the system user has some knowledge of the information that is actually stored. For example, in the library catalogue system the user must know that date information is kept. The user of such a system must also know how to ask the system questions. These requirements restrict the use of data base systems to those who have had some training in how to make use of the system.

With very few exceptions indeed, all government departments, local authorities, and commercial/industrial concerns are totally dependent on their data bases for continuing their business. All information which pertains to the business is stored on some kind of computer system whether that information is criminal records, staff employed, customer details, or whatever.

Whilst many of these data bases are organised in an incompatible way, in some cases they can exchange information. For instance, police computers are normally able to access driver and vehicle licencing computers so that the police can find out about suspect cars and drivers.

In theory, it is possible to link many different data bases and relate information on a single person or thing stored in different computer systems. Whilst this facility is sometimes useful, it can pose problems and this leads us on to what is one of the most outstanding areas of social concern about computers – the maintenance of privacy.

2.5 THE PRIVACY PROBLEM

The privacy problem is probably the most immediate computer-related social problem which must be solved. The privacy problem is the problem of how to develop safeguards so that personal privacy is maintained in the face of universal computerisation, computer communications, and the maintenance of very large data bases of personal information.

The storage of personal information is not new. Medical records, employee records, tax records, etc. have been kept for many years by local government, national government and by private industry. There has always been a privacy problem inasmuch as unauthorised access to this information had to be disallowed. Before computerisation, the information had to be accessed via a file clerk or secretary who knew who was and wasn't allowed access to the information. The information was safely locked away when the file clerk was unavailable.

Furthermore, although the information maintained is no different, it was maintained in geographically distinct places and it was practically impossible to correlate that information. Given an individual's car number say, it was only possible to access vehicle information, given a tax number, tax information, etc. There was no way that access to one file of information would permit follow-through access to any other information files.

Now, the advent of computerised data base systems has removed some of these checks which are an inherent part of manual filing systems. Given appropriate communications equipment, computers can be accessed by telephone from anywhere in the world. There is no need for this access to go through some human agency – it can be completely automatic.

Correlation of data can also be automated. It is now feasible to search through millions of entries in a data base looking for a particular entry. The ordering of the records in the data base is irrelevant. If an item of information such as an address can be obtained from one data base, this address can be used to find the corresponding items in other data bases.

As more and more data is stored and processed on a computer, there has been an unfortunate tendency by some agencies to collect data for no particular reason except that it might conceivably be useful in future. This was previously impossible because manual filing systems are expensive to organise whereas the addition of extra information to a record in a data base is relatively cheap.

Of course, the general problem of maintaining privacy rights is not just a problem of computerisation. It also relates to the control of surveillance (bugging) equipment, the control of what information an individual might reasonable be expected to provide to government agencies, employers, hospitals, etc., and the control of the mass media. Unquestionably, some elements of the mass media have been guilty of privacy intrusions - taking secret photographs or interviewing people who are not physically or emotionally fit enough to provide properly considered responses.

Space does not permit a full discussion of the general problem of preserving privacy. It is not possible to discuss questions such as controlling bugging, the responsibility of the mass media or even controlling data collection. Rather,I shall confine the discussion here to those issues which are directly related to the storage of information in data base systems and the abuse of such information.

2.5.1 The abuse of data base systems

The problem of controlling illegal or unwarranted access to systems which store personal information is not, in itself, a direct consequence of maintaining these systems on a computer. However, computerising such systems vastly magnifies the problem because it makes the information so much more readily available and because the computer can process the information and come to conclusions on the basis of that information. In this section, I shall describe some of the different kinds of privacy violation which may occur when computers are used for keeping personal information.

These violations fall into four classes:

(1)   Violations due to incorrect personal information being disseminated and actions taken on the basis of that information.

(2)   Violations due to information falling into the wrong hands.

(3)   Violations due to information being passed to some agency which was not originally responsible for collecting that information.

(4)   Violations due to information being used for some purpose which is distinct from that for which it was originally collected.

The most serious violations are generally a result of the combination of factors 1 and 2. That is, if incorrect information is passed to individuals or organisations who have no right to such information.

A well-publicised case of this type occurred a few years ago in the UK. A member of a (British) film crew on location in Europe was mistakenly identified as a member of an urban terrorist group. The local police passed this information to the police in the UK where it was stored in a national criminal intelligence computer system.

Some time later, the individual in question was refused a job for no specific reason. Fortunately, she discovered later that the firm who refused here had had unwarranted access to the police computer system. On finding out that the job applicant was a suspected terrorist, they (understandably) refused her the job.

Fortunately, in this case, the individual concerned had personal connections with the police and was able to get the incorrect information changed. However, without these connections (which most of us don't have), it is very unlikely that the incorrect information would have been corrected or even detected.

This particular case raises a number of general questions:

(1)   Should individuals be allowed to see information which is stored on computer data base systems about themselves?

(2)   What mechanism can be derived to correct that information if it is wrong?

(3)   Are the security procedures associated with the police and similar computer systems adequate? If so, is it general practice to release information from such systems to outside organisations?

I shall attempt to provide some answers to the first two of these questions in the following section. As for the question of computer system security, there is increasing evidence, in the UK at least, that the security procedures associated with government computer systems are inadequate and that it is not uncommon for information from such systems to be released to outside organisations.

Two further anecdotes, both concerning British members of parliament, illustrate this. In early 1982, an MP introduced a Private Member's bill in parliament which proposed legislation to control computerised data base systems holding personal information. A few days after this was announced, a popular newspaper illustrated the need for control by publishing many

personal details about that MP such as financial
information, criminal record (he had none), car licence
information, etc. Much of this information could only
have been obtained from police, government, and private
data base systems. Leaving aside the question of
whether the newspaper itself was guilty of privacy
violations by actually publishing this information, it
clearly illustrates that much so-called confidential
information is readily available to anyone willing to
pay for it.

The same year, another MP paid for petrol by credit
card. The service station staff failed to operate the
card recording machine correctly and his card number
was not properly recorded. However, the staff had
noted his car registration number. Subsequently, the
government vehicle licencing computer was used to trace
the MP in order that he might pay for the petrol. His
investigations of how he could have been traced
disclosed that for trivially small fee, information
from this data base system would be given to anyone who
had 'reasonable cause'. It was not made clear what
constituted a 'reasonable cause' and how the integrity
of those requiring the information was checked.

These examples of misuse of government data base
systems raise two more questions:

(1)   What safeguards can be built into computer sys-
       tems themselves to prevent disclosure of informa-
       tion to unauthorised persons?

(2)   Should personal information from government com-
       puter systems be made available to ANY outside,
       private organisation?

Let us now look at privacy violations which fall
into classes 3 and 4 discussed above, namely those due
to information being passed around and information
being used for some purpose distinct from that for
which it was originally collected.

Probably the most irritating consequence of
information being passed around (usually it is sold) is
the incredible amount of 'junk mail' we all seem to
receive nowadays. For instance, say you buy a fairly
expensive piece of electronic equipment such as a hi-fi
system and, in good faith, fill in and post the
guarantee card which usually comes with such systems.
The makers of the system now have your name and address
and know you to be a person of good taste - at least as
far as hi-fi systems are concerned. Having collected a
list of names and addresses of buyers of their system,
this list could then be sold to record clubs and you
might receive advertising from them. The record clubs
could sell the list to book clubs, and you'd get junk

mail from them. The chain might continue almost indefinitely with the junk mail becoming less and less related to hi-fi systems.

This hypothetical situation illustrates both privacy violations described above. Firstly, the information is not being used for the purpose for which it was collected (the maintenance of guarantees) and secondly, the information is being passed to all sorts of other organisations (record clubs, book clubs, etc.). There are, therefore, two further questions to be added to our list:

(1)   Should personal information be passed around or sold without the permission of the person in question?

(2)   Should it be permitted that information collected for some clearly defined purpose be used for some other purpose without permission?

There have been many publicised examples due to the abuse of data base systems apart from those which have been described here. It is reasonable to conjecture, furthermore, that these publicised examples are only the very tip of the iceberg. There are almost certainly very many more violations that have gone unpublicised.

The dangers associated with computerised personal information have already been recognised in many countries and they have introduced controlling legislation of one kind or another. It is my opinion that most of this legislation is inadequate in one respect or another and, in the next section, I shall describe the safeguards which ought to be built into any 'data protection' legislation.

2.5.2 Controlling personal information systems

Recall that in the previous section, a number of questions were posed concerning the control which ought to be exerted over computerised stores of personal information. These questions were:

(1)   Should people be allowed access to their own personal records?

(2)   How can they ensure that this information is corrected if it is incorrect?

(3)   How can we stop this information being disclosed to private organisations?

(4)   Should the sale of personal information be permitted?

(5)   Should it be permitted that information collected
      for one purpose be used in some completely dif-
      ferent way?

There are no simple answers to these questions and some
of them relate directly to the rights of an individual
in society. Inevitably, any safeguards which are
introduced are not without cost - and a further
question must be posed. What is an acceptable price to
pay for personal privacy?

      Some would argue that governmental and commercial
convenience is paramount and that the existence of
restrictions (safeguards) would make the job of
government more difficult and would reduce the
competitiveness of commercial organisations. Whilst
this may indeed be true, it is hardly a good reason for
not having such safeguards. After all, if commercial
convenience is taken as paramount, employers would not
have to provide safe working conditions. The analogy
is clear - the individual has to be protected from
commercial convenience.

      In this section, we shall look at answers to the
questions above from both technical and legislative
viewpoints. I shall describe the notion of data
protection and discuss how individual privacy can be
maintained.

      The first, important, point that must be made is
that computer systems are potentially much more secure
than manual systems. It is possible to build in
security features to data base systems so that access
to the system is completely forbidden to unauthorised
individuals. Some examples of these technical features
are:

(1)   Information can be stored in a coded, unreadable
      form. Only those authorised to access the infor-
      mation are provided with a key to break the code.
      Using this key, the information can be converted
      to readable form, by the computer, when an au-
      thorised access is made.

(2)   Each and every access to any information can be
      recorded along with details of the individual who
      made that access. This would make undetected ac-
      cess impossible and would deter casual nosiness -
      browsing through personal information.

(3)   A password might be associated with each record
      in the system. In order to examine a record, the
      user would have to provide the password associat-
      ed with that particular record. Without this
      password, access to the record would be forbid-
      den.

All of these, and other security features, are

technically realisable now but are rarely implemented except on the most secure military systems. The reason for this is that the inclusion of such safeguards in a computer system significantly increases the price of that system. Where there is no predefined requirements that security features should be included in a system, commercial considerations dictate that such features will be left out.

All these technical safeguards are designed to prevent unauthorised access to a data base but there is considerable evidence to suggest that many privacy violations are due to information being accessed by authorised persons. They are either careless in whom they disclose the information to or are corrupt and sell the information. For instance, in a recent UK court case, a policeman was convicted of taking money in return for confidential information from the police national computer.

Watertight technical safeguards to prevent such access are virtually impossible to implement. Almost all of our social systems are dependent on the integrity of the individuals who are part of the system and computer based systems are no exception to this.

One possible safeguard which might deter abuses of this type is to record the reason for the access to the data base as well as the name of the person retrieving the information, the time, and the place of access. This would enable some checking to be carried out and would probably deter careless disclosure of information. It is unlikely, however, that this alone would prevent deliberate abuses by those users who were authorised to access information held in the data base.

As well as technical safeguards, there must be associated 'data protection' legislation which should clearly set out the rights of the individual with respect to computerised personal information, which should define the limits of usage of personal information and which should establish penalties for those who abuse personal information systems.

Features which ought to be included in data protection legislation are:

(1) Every organisation which wished to maintain personal information should have to apply for a licence to do so. This licence should only be granted if the organisation could show that it maintained reasonable security over its data.

(2) Every company, government department, etc. who maintain personal information systems should have to declare this fact and a central, public, register of personal information data bases should be maintained. This would allow people to find out which organisations actually kept computerised records of their personal details.

(3)   Any individual should have the right to inspect his own records on any system.

(4)   If the information in these records is verifiably incorrect, the organisation keeping these records must correct them. Furthermore, the organisation must ensure that any copies of the records which are kept elsewhere are also corrected.

(5)   It should be forbidden for commercial organisations to sell information about individuals without the permission of the individual concerned.

(6)   For all personal information which is maintained, information about the source of that information must be maintained. This would allow the original version of the incorrect information to be traced and corrected.

(7)   If information is transferred to some other data base for any reason, a record of the destination must be kept. This would allow all copies of incorrect information to be found and corrected.

(8)   It should be forbidden for organisations to use personal information for some purpose distinct from that for which it was collected without the permission of the individual involved.

(9)   It should be forbidden for government agencies to disclose information to any non-governmental organisations.

(10)   If any organisation is found to be circumventing data protection legislation, its licence to hold personal information should be revoked.

(11)   A data protection authority, funded by the taxpayer, should be set up to enforce data protection legislation. This authority should be completely independent, like the judiciary, and should be able to impose sanctions on those who do not comply with data protection legislation.

There are two main arguments which are sometimes put forward in opposition to such safeguards. Firstly, some systems, such as police computer systems, would lose much of their effectiveness if the information held in these systems were to be disclosed. Secondly, some commercial organisations argue that disclosing information and maintaining proper records puts them at a commercial disadvantage. This is particularly acute when the organisation's competitors from another

country are not subject to data protection legislation.
The first or these arguments can be met by allowing systems to seek exemption from the public release of information. Rather than individuals having access to the information held on these systems, access must be made through a data auditor. This individual should be an independent arbiter, such as a member of the judiciary, who should perform periodic and random checks on these systems to ensure that the information held there is correct. Furthermore, if a member of the public feels that incorrect information is held on such a system, he or she should be able to ask the data auditor to have the particular record checked and corrected if necessary.

The second argument against data protection is more difficult to refute. There will probably always be countries where the rights of the individual are not properly recognised and businesses in these countries do have commercial advantages. At the moment, it is common for multinational companies to divert some of their operations to Third World countries who do not have stringent safety legislation and where it is common to pay subsistence level wages. Because such places exist does not mean that the rights of the individual should not be protected. On moral grounds alone, personal privacy should be a statutory right.

Some kind of data protection legislation has been introduced in many countries. In the UK, minimal data protection legislation is proposed but not (at the time of writing) implemented.

The problems of maintaining personal privacy in a world where more and more information is held on computer systems are complex and difficult to solve. However, this does not mean that they should be ignored in the hope that they will go away. There is a real need for technical security safeguards to be a statutory part of computer systems and for complete and thorough legislation governing the operation of systems which store personal information.

2.6   SUMMARY

This chapter has concentrated on the nature of information, the storage of large amounts of information on computers and at some of the problems which result from maintaining files of personal information on computer systems.

Videotex and teletext systems are new ways of using television where the TV set becomes a kind of computer terminal where text can be displayed. In a teletext system, text is transmitted, by the TV companies, in parallel with normal TV programs. The viewer can switch between teletext and any other programme. A videotex system, on the other hand, makes use of a telephone line to connect the viewer's TV set to a central computer. Using the system, he or she has access to thousands of pages of information.

A virtue of videotex systems is that they use a very simple, easily understood, way of storing their information. This means that users of these systems need no special training. Within a few minutes of getting started, they can make effective use of the system. However, the simple organisation does have many drawbacks and data base systems have been developed to provide more general facilities for storing and manipulating large volumes of information.

Data base systems are computer systems which are explicitly designed to handle very large volumes of information. They require the user to have some knowledge of what information is stored and how it is represented in the system. Because of this, they are not really suitable for use by casual users but the flexible data organisation makes some kinds of information retrieval very straightforward indeed. Data base systems are now an integral part of the administration of commercial and governmental organisations.

The facility to store, process, and retrieve very large amounts of information means that personal files such as criminal records, bank account records, etc. are now frequently maintained on a computer system. In itself, this should increase efficiency but it does mean that new safeguards have to be devised to prevent personal information being divulged to unauthorised persons. Computers can readily search through thousands of personal records and can correlate records held in different data bases. This offers enormous scope for violations of personal privacy and one of the most pressing problems which we have today is to ensure that an individuals right to privacy is maintained in the face of universal computerisation.

This right can really only be protected by legislation. Governments should introduce data protection laws which allow individuals to check that the information held on personal files is correct. These laws should also include mechanisms so that erroneous information may be corrected and organisations who abuse the data protection laws should be penalised.

Chapter 3
The everyday computer

Microprocessors in one form of another will pervade all aspects of everyday life. We will be wakened in the morning by a microprocessor controlled alarm clock and cook breakfast on a microprocessor controlled cooker. In fact, we may even be able to program our cooker so that some of our breakfast is already cooked for us when we get up. We shall travel to work in vehicles – cars, buses, trains – which incorporate a number of microprocessors. Many of us will use computers at work. At home in the evening, we will watch microprocessor controlled television, use a home computer or use microprocessor controlled tools in our hobbies. Whilst we are out, machines, controlled by microprocessors, will wash clothes and, perhaps, will automatically clean floors for us.

The idea of a home computer is one that has only become realisable with the advent of the microprocessor. Before large scale integration, the fabrication and assembly costs of a computer were such that these machines could only be afforded by large organisations and government departments. The idea of having a computer system at home or of using a computer as a controller of household devices such as washing machines and cookers was ridiculous.

Now costs of computers have fallen to such an extent that it is possible to buy a small computer, to be used in conjunction with a TV set, for about the same price as a reasonably high quality portable radio. For a few hundred pounds or dollars, you can buy quite a sophisticated computer system offering colour graphics and audio output.

As far as everyday uses of the computer are concerned, the invention of the microchip is comparable with the development of small, low-power electric motors. As small electric motors developed from industrial motors, they were included in more and more domestic devices such as vacuum cleaners, refrigerators (to drive a pump), lawnmowers, etc. In a typical modern household there are probably somewhere between 10 and 20 machines which incorporate low power electric motors. For example, in my home the following devices have electric motors – vacuum cleaner, refrigerator, heating system, record deck, tape deck, portable cassette recorder, liquidiser, food processor, lawnmower, and power drill. In a few years, there will be as many microprocessors in the home as there are electric motors.

Because computers are so small and cheap, it is now sensible to use microelectronic devices as controllers in anything which needs in-built control. This means that complex, potentially unreliable, electro-mechanical controls in washing machines, cookers, heating systems, etc. are now being replaced by all-electronic controls. Not only are these electronic controllers much cheaper, they are also more reliable as they have no moving parts.

In future, electronic controllers will be incorporated into all sorts of devices which presently have only simple manual controls. For example, an electric drill may include a controller chip to monitor the drill speed and vary that speed according to the material being drilled. At the moment, a manual switch is used to change drill speeds and the user has the option of two or at most three different speeds.

Computer systems will also be an integral part of almost all vehicles. Already, aircraft are flown largely by computer. New subway and rapid transport systems in Europe and the USA have been designed to run driverless trains under computer control. Computers are now appearing in automobiles, mostly in the role of providing better instrumentation but, in a few cars, taking over engine control functions.

The availability of cheap computer systems and the fact that a large number of people will use a computer at work will mean that our conventional thinking on education will have to change. Education in computing will become an essential part of elementary schooling. The use of computers will change the teaching of other subjects such as physics, mathematics, languages, and geography. Furthermore, educational opportunities will no longer be confined, almost exclusively, to the young. Because of the rapidly changing nature of society, adult education will become the norm with everyone learning several skills on the course of their life. This means that there will be increasing demands made on the educational system and to satisfy these demands, educationalists will have to make use of information technology.

In the last chapter, we saw some examples of how computers will become involved in everyday life through teletext and cable television systems. With these systems, the user usually makes use of a fairly large computer and communications equipment to interchange information with that machine. In this chapter, I shall concentrate on small computer systems and their uses in various common everyday situations.

Firstly, we shall look at the uses of personal computers in the home and then I shall describe how the computer can be used as a controller incorporated into domestic devices like washing machines and cookers. I then go on to describe how education will be revolutionised by information technology. The widespread use of computers in the home and in education is likely to have profound social effects — some of these are discussed in this chapter. A fuller discussion of long term social implications is provided in Chapter 8.

3.1 COMPUTERS IN THE HOME

Along with video tape recorders, personal computers are now one of the boom areas of consumer electronics. There are now hundreds of thousands of people who have their own personal microcomputer. In general, they make use of an ordinary TV set to provide output for the user and are really remarkable value for money. It is possible to buy a programmable home computer with a audio output device and which can generate colour graphics on a TV screen for the price of a stereo amplifier. Ten years ago, a comparable system would have cost at least 100 times today's price.

There are an increasing number of people who have a microprocessor in their home but don't actually realise it. This system is built into some other device such as a cooker or a dishwasher and acts a a machine controller. The role of the microprocessor as a controller is described later in this chapter.

The major use of home, personal computers at the moment is recreational — they are used to play games. However, many users are also becoming computer hobbyists and learning to write their own computer programs. In some cases, they become very proficient indeed and write impressive and complex applications programs.

It seems likely that the use of personal computers as rather sophisticated toys will remain the most common application of home computers. Within a remarkably short time, computer games have developed from simple bat and ball games, like tennis, to complex simulations of battles, treasure hunts, or space wars. These games are often extremely addictive, even to the most cynical computer professionals. An even more sophisticated games are invented, the attractiveness of the computer as a toy will increase.

Just as most people who own a camera do not take photography very seriously, most owners of home computers will simply use them to play games or, perhaps, for very simple applications such as maintaining lists of one kind or another. However, just as there is a large number of keen amateur photographers, there will be a fairly large number of computer hobbyists who enjoy inventing computer programs for various applications.

Although these hobbyists will invent useful programs, and advertisers will trumpet the virtues of a personal computer for household management, there are actually few everyday tasks which are made significantly easier by using a computer. Hobbyists will devise programs for all manner of things from looking after the weekly shopping list to household budget calculations but most of these simple chores are really best done with a pencil, paper and, maybe, a pocket calculator. Lists on the kitchen wall are probably a more effective way of running a household than an all singing, dancing, and whistling computer program.

Household management tasks don't really need a computer but one important and potentially valuable use of a home machine is as an educational 'toy' for children of all ages. Even pre-school children can learn a lot from a computer as long as it can draw them pictures and make attractive sounds. Older children can learn to program the machine and can make use of it for computer-assisted learning. Although most of these children will never be professional computer scientists, familiarity with a home computer will mean that they do not have the awe and fear of computer systems which is common in so many older people.

The notions of interactive television and teletext systems has already been introduced in Chapter 2. The usefulness of these systems can be increased if they are used in conjunction with a personal computer. As well as being displayed on the TV screen, teletext information can also be 'captured' by a home computer, stored in its memory and subsequently processed in some way.

One important consequence of this is that the distribution of computer programs will be vastly simplified. At the moment, if someone has a program to sell, that program must be made available in some form (such as a cassette tape or floppy disk) which is shared by both the buyer and the seller of the program. As there are few media standards, most personal computers use different ways of recording information on tape or floppy disk. It is not usually possible to take a program prepared for one type of computer and use it on another type of machine. This means that, program sellers have to prepare different versions of their program for different machines.

This situation can be simplified by making use of a videotex system for distributing programs. Sellers of programs, such as games or other programs for hobbyists, can put these programs onto a number of videotex pages to be accessed by the buyer. To collect his copy, the buyer connects his home computer to the videotex system and accesses the appropriate pages. These are copied to his own computer's memory and his machine automatically converts them from videotex form to the form used by that particular computer.

Payment for programs is also easy to organise with such a system. As a charge can be associated with each videotex page, the cost of the program is simply the cost of accessing these pages. It is added to the user's videotex account and subsequently forwarded to the seller of the program.

Similarly, programs could be broadcast using teletext systems. Experimental trials of such broadcasting have already been undertaken so that television series for computer hobbyists could include programs to be run on a home machine.

Another possible use of home computers connected to a videotex system is the establishment of an electronic mail service. To send information to some other user of the system requires that the information be typed and stored on the sender's computer. This is then connected to a videotex system where each user has his or her own mail box. Forwarding information involves transferring it from the sender's computer to the receiver's mail box. When the recipient of the mail next uses the system, he is told that mail is available.

Of course there are some problems with this. For a start, there is no way that the sender could be sure that the recipient got his mail. Occasional videotex users might not use the system for weeks on end so that it would not be useful for any kind of urgent mail. Furthermore, such a system opens up horrendous opportunities for senders of junk mail. Advertisers, mail-order companies, etc. could broadcast mail to every user's mail box. Genuine mail could easily be discarded accidentally amidst the floods of such rubbish.

Fortunately, the clever home computer user could eliminate some of the junk mail automatically. Rather than read his or her mail directly, the user could first pass it to his own computer for sorting. This machine could be programmed with the names of friends so that mail from them could be selected from the junk. Furthermore, it could also be programmed to scan the mail and recognise phrases such as 'fabulous offer', 'unrepeatable bargain' or 'chance of a lifetime' and automatically discard these items.

A spin-off from connecting a personal computer to a teletext system is that information presented in the text pages can be collected by the computer and presented in a form which is more amenable to human readers. We have already seen that the amount of text in a teletext page is quite small. A personal computer could collect the text from a number of pages, put it together then print it in some compact and readable way.

So far, this section has concentrated on the active use of home computers but most people will have lots of computers around their home without them knowing anything about it. These will be built into other devices and one of their functions will be to act as device controllers. Another function which we shall describe here is to provide information about the state of a device either visually or as speech output.

Many household devices include some kind of state indicator which shows how they are set up or how they are operating. For example, a cooker might include a dial to set oven temperatures and an indicator light which shows when the oven has reached the correct temperature. A camera might have a viewfinder display indicating whether its controls are set for the correct exposure and a radio has a dial to show the station which has been selected.

The microprocessor which controls the display would normally be directly connected to the microprocessor built into the machine controller. Information from the controller would be passed directly to the display processor so that comprehensive, up-to-date state information would be immediately available. Usually, this information would be shown on a digital display although more complex devices, such as a video recorder, might include a small TV-like screen for providing information about the state of the machine.

Rather than on-off warning lights, computer controlled displays will be able to show the exact state of a device at any particular instant. As the oven heats up, its actual temperature will be shown. The shutter speed and aperture selected by the camera user will be displayed in the viewfinder and radios will show the station frequency on a digital display. Some systems like this are already available and they will become more and more common in future.

In time, some machines may even incorporate speech output devices where computer-generated speech will tell the user the state of the system. The workings of such speech output systems are discussed in Chapter 7.

Using speech output, the cooker might tell the housewife that the oven has reached the desired temperature or might remind her that the oven needs cleaning. A speech device built into a car could warn the driver and passengers to fasten safety belts or that speed limits were being exceeded.

Although technically possible now, speech output devices have the disadvantage that they can be very aggravating, particularly if they are designed to repeat information incessantly. For this reason, they may not be built in to many household devices in case they discourage people from buying these machines.

In the same way as developments like electric power and television have had far-reaching effects on society, so too will the universal use of computers in everyday situations. These developments will not occur in isolation but in the context of a world economic situation which is such that it is unlikely that existing industrial economies will experience high growth rates. There will only be small increases in the real income of the population. Governments are likely to continue to restrict spending in order that inflation be constrained and, in the long term, energy prices are likely to rise faster than the rate of inflation.

Because of this economic situation and also because of widespread automation in industry and commerce, unemployment in the industrialised countries is likely to be high. Crime is likely to increase. There will be less money for travel and life is likely to become more and more home-centred particularly in suburban areas. There will be many computerised systems developed to support this home-centred way of life.

We have already seen how dozens if not hundreds of television channels can be made available via satellites and cable. In conjunction with pre-recorded video cassettes and disks as well as computer games, there will be no shortage of home entertainment.

Homes are likely to be protected with computerised security systems and it will be possible to order much of the weekly shopping through videotex and have it delivered to your home. Personal communication will be possible through videotex systems and other computer conferencing networks which will allow groups to confer without being in the same place.

The net result of this home-centred existence is likely to be increasing social isolation with families only having personal contacts with immediate friends and relatives. This social isolation could put pressure on the nuclear family unit. It will lead to an increased number of marriage breakdowns, child abuse and so on. Social isolation is also likely to lead to decreased tolerance for minority groups and, possibly, an increase in those supporting extremist political groups. The reason for this is simply that people will have less and less contact with minority groups as they spend more and more time at home and with a small circle of friends. Because of the lack of contact, they will not understand the differences between the different groups in the population.

3.2   THE CONTROLLING COMPUTER

Many everyday devices incorporate some kind of simple control system which can be used to partially automate their operation. For example, cookers often incorporate a timer which can be set to switch the

58

cooker on and off. Heating systems have a linked timer and thermostat control, and washing machines have 'programmes' for different kinds of fabric and wash temperatures. Until very recently, these simple controllers were electro-mechanical in nature but with the advent of VLSI and the invention of the microprocessor, these electro-mechanical systems are being replaced by all-electronic computerised controllers. The operation of the machine is are governed by a computer program which sets out how the controller should react to the various situations which it is designed deal with.

There are a number of benefits gained by using an electronic rather than an electro-mechanical controller. The most important of these are:

(1)   Microprocessor-based controllers are cheaper than electro-mechanical controllers because they are a good deal simpler and have many fewer parts than their electro-mechanical equivalent.

(2)   Because of the complexity of electro-mechanical controllers, they are inherently less reliable than electronic controllers with no moving parts.

(3)   As the decisions made by a computerised controller are made by a program, the capabilities of the controller can be changed by changing its program. This means that the same basic controller can be incorporated in different devices with a different control program for each device. Furthermore, design changes in a device can often be accommodated simply by changing the control program but without changes to the controller itself.

Computers have been used as controllers since the mid-sixties when the minicomputer was invented specifically for this function. However, minicomputers are relatively bulky and expensive so can only be used in large complex systems such as chemical process plants, power stations, etc. Microprocessors, on the other hand, are so small and cheap that they can replace existing controllers and can be included in devices which previously had only manual control.

Computerised controllers rely on sensors, such as temperature sensors, to gather information about their environment and normally incorporate a clock for timing. They can change the state of their environment by sending control signals to other devices such as pumps, motors, etc.

A schematic representation of this is shown in Figure 3.1.

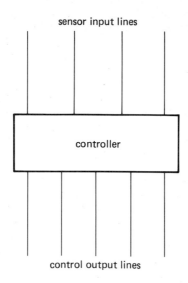

sensor input lines

controller

control output lines

Fig. 3.1   A schematic computerised controller

The sensors connected to the controller each monitor
some single environmental parameter such as
temperature, flow of liquid in a pipe, distortion of a
beam, etc. Decisions are made by the controller on the
basis of its sensory input and control signals issued
as necessary. Because the computer is so fast, it
normally operates simply by looking at each sensor at
regular intervals – say about 10 times every second. In
most domestic devices, events don't usually happen that
quickly, so this gives the machine plenty of time to
respond to any particular situation.

The control program which is built into the
microprocessor is simply a set of instructions
specifying which control signals are to be issued at
different times and sensor settings. For example,
consider a simple program which might be part of a
washing machine control program. This part of the
program is intended to control the filling of a drum
with water at a particular temperature. It has two
sensor inputs – one determining if the drum is full and
the other checking water temperature. It has four
lines sending control signals – to a switch which opens
and closes a cold water valve, to the corresponding hot
water valve switch, to a heater switch, and to a
warning light switch. The machine may have other
sensors and control lines but these are not relevant to
this example.

A schematic diagram of this is shown in Figure 3.2.

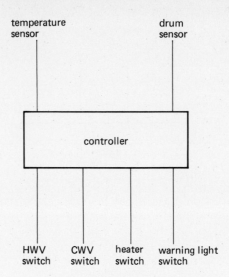

Fig. 3.2   A washing machine control system

The control program which fills the drum with water
at the right temperature works by mixing hot and cold
water till the drum is full. If the temperature is too
low at this point, it switches on a heater. If the
temperature is too high, it causes a warning light to
come on and waits for the water to cool of its own
accord. This latter situation is quite unlikely as too
high a temperature after filling would mean that the
ambient cold water temperature was too high. However,
the system detects high temperatures and warns the user
because it could mean that there was some kind of fault
in the machine.

The working of this program is described below, in a
non-technical way, as an **algorithm**. An algorithm is
simply a set of instructions setting out exactly how to
go about some task. Establishing the algorithm is the
first step in devising a computer program. Once the
exact requirements have been set out it is usually
quite easy to translate them into a computer
programming language, like BASIC , which can be
understood by the machine. In the description of the
washing machine control algorithm below, the following
conventions have been adopted.

(1)   The keywords if and otherwise indicate conditions
       and alternatives.

(2)   The keyword repeat means that actions have to be
       repeated one or more times.

(3)   Actions which are indented by the same number of
       spaces group together in the same way as bracket-
       ing can group parts of mathematical expressions.

The control program is:

```
1.   Open hot water valve (HWV)
2.   Open cold water valve (CWV)
3.   repeat 10 times per second
3.1      if drum sensor indicates 'FULL'
            close HWV and CWV
            go to step 4
3.2      otherwise
3.2.1       if temperature is 'HIGH'
            close HWV
            if CWV is closed
               open CWV
3.2.2       otherwise
               if temperature is 'LOW'
                  close CWV
                  if HWV is closed
                     open HWV
3.3      go back to step 3
4.   if temperature is 'LOW'
4.1      switch on heater
4.2      repeat 10 times per second
            if temperature is 'HIGH'
               switch off heater
               go to step 5
4.3      go back to step 4.2
5.   switch on warning light
6.   repeat 10 times per second
6.1      if temperature is not 'HIGH'
            switch off warning light
            go to step 7
6.2      go back to step 6
7.   ....
```

The controller first opens both control valves to fill
the drum. Step 3 in the sequence is then repeated
until the drum is full, with the temperature sensors
governing whether the hot water or cold water valves
should be opened. Once the drum is full, step 4 in the
sequence is activated to bring the water up to the
correct temperature, if necessary, by switching on the
heater. Once the temperature sensor indicates that the
water is hot enough control passes to step 5. Notice
that the warning light is always switched on but is
immediately switched off if the water temperature is
correct. If the temperature is too high, however, the
light remains on and control does not move to the next
part of the program at step 7.
    The introduction of computerised controllers into
everyday devices is already underway. Microprocessor

controlled cookers, washing machines, cameras, etc. are already on the market and many more computerised products are planned. Some cars now incorporate computerised fuel control in the carburettor which provide greater fuel economy and in future more and more automobile functions will be controlled by computer.

Examples of computerised control systems which have already been built into some automobiles or which are planned are cruise controllers where the driver sets a cruising speed and it is automatically maintained, anti-skid braking controllers which switch the car brakes on and off very quickly to prevent the wheels locking, and automatic gear controllers which provide continuous automatic transmission, adjusting the gear to the speed of the car and the load on the engine.

In future, it may even be possible to build an automatic car driver which could take over car driving on certain routes. This would involve building position indicators into the road and incorporating sensors into the car which could read these indicators. Other sensors, perhaps based on radar, could detect other cars. The car autodriver would use the input from these sensors to adjust the car's speed and road position without intervention from the driver.

The advantages of such a system are obvious. Accidents would be reduced as autodrivers wouldn't fall asleep or make mistakes. Speed limits in towns and restrictions due to weather or road conditions could be automatically enforced. Average speeds would be increased because traffic could bunch more closely together without risk of accident.

Of course, such a system will never be universal. The cost of equipping minor roads with position indicators is not economically justifiable, considering the number of vehicles which use them. Driverless cars are not, therefore, a real future possibility. However, the system could certainly be installed in cities and in major cross-cross country routes. In cities, the existence of such a system would mean that driverless, completely automatic public transport systems would be possible.

3.3 INFORMATION TECHNOLOGY AND EDUCATION

The industrial revolution of the 18th and 19th centuries had a great number of long-term effects. One of the most important of these was the effect on education. Because the new machinery used in factories was relatively sophisticated, operators had to be educated to a higher standard than was previously necessary for a population who were predominantly peasant farmworkers. Ultimately, the needs of industry resulted in universal education and a population, in the industrialised countries, which is now almost 100% literate.

Now, new information technology is placing further demands on the educational system. Not only must future users of information technology be able to read, write and count, they must also be 'computer literate' - able to make use of a computer in their everyday life.

We shall look at how educational systems must adapt to provide computer literacy, how information technology itself is likely to change educational methods and we shall consider some of the problems and consequences of computerising education.

3.3.1 Computer literacy

It has been estimated that, by 1995, over a third of the working population will make direct use of computers in their work. Roughly the same proportion will indirectly use computers built into other systems. This means that there is a need for a tremendous educational effort to establish a foundation on which further training in particular uses of computers can be built. This foundation is comparable with the basic skills of reading and writing so the term 'computer literacy' has been coined to describe it.

Unfortunately, many educational administrators and some teachers are obviously confused by the speed of developments in information technology and equate 'computer literacy' with computer programming. Accordingly, schools are installing microcomputer systems and pressure is being put on them to establish classes in computer programming. Hasty decisions on equipment provision and teaching methods are being made which may ultimately exacerbate many of the misconceptions about computers which are now common. In fact, concentrating on education in computer programming could alienate a large sector of the population from computers.

The fundamental problem with basing elementary computer education on computer programming is that existing, widely available programming languages like BASIC are not really adequate for expressing solutions for anything but the most trivial numeric problems. As a result, programming a computer to do useful things is a difficult, intellectually demanding task which takes a long time.

This means that, in schools, computer programming is seen as an activity for academically oriented students and those which are less intellectually gifted sometimes see computers as difficult to use, unsympathetic, and something to be feared. This is unfortunate as properly written computer systems can make the machine easy to use and rewarding for even the least academic students. In fact, experiments at

Edinburgh University have demonstrated that the communication skills of autistic children can be dramatically improved by allowing them to play with properly designed computer programs.

The notion of computer literacy as described above is based on the assumption that computer hardware is a general purpose tool and that effective use of this tool requires that the user needs to know how to write control programs. This is certainly true as far as professional computer scientists are concerned but the majority of the population will never have any need to program a microcomputer. Rather, they will use the computer for particular applications such as word processing, financial processing, or machine control and pre-written programs will come with the machine to tailor it to the needs of each user.

What is needed to achieve computer literacy is educational programmes which demonstrate the range of applications of computers and show how the computer can carry out many repetitive tasks more efficiently than humans. Furthermore, it must be shown that computers need not be difficult to use, are not necessarily unfriendly, do not require high intellectual skills to understand, and need not always be instructed in the arcane symbols of programming languages such as BASIC or PASCAL.

Elementary computer education should also discuss the limitations of computers and how they can complement human skills. They ought to provide students with direct experience of using computers to solve problems rather than programming computers in a trivial way. Finally, computer education should prepare students for the society of the future by discussing social changes which are likely to result from universal computerisation.

Of course, there is a role for the teaching of computer programming in schools. This role is as a subsidiary rather than a dominant part of computer education courses and it should, perhaps, be optional. One useful skill which programming can demonstrate is that problem are not solved on their first attempt but that many attempts are needed to move towards the final solution. Computer programs are excellent vehicles for this demonstration as they are invariably incorrect at first and must go through a process of debugging — correcting errors until a correct program is attained.

In summary then, probably the most pressing educational need of the 1980s is the establishment of courses in elementary computer studies so that universal 'computer literacy' can be achieved. These courses should not be based on computer programming but should provide a broader appreciation of computers and information technology and must be tailored to suit both academic and non-academic students.

3.3.2 Computerised education

Apart from education in computing and related aspects of information technology, the teaching of all other subjects is likely to be influenced by information technology. There are various reasons for this.

(1)   The technology can improve the educational process, making many topics easier to understand.

(2)   There will be commercial pressures trying to sell the technology to the large market offered by educational establishments.

(3)   There will be financial pressures on education to increase teacher productivity and reduce costs without decreasing standards.

All this will occur in the face of greatly increased educational demand caused by the need for retraining people to work with information technology.

We shall look at some of the potential uses of information technology in education here. These include computer-assisted learning, the use of educational television, teletext systems in education and remote-learning programmes. I shall also describe some of the disadvantages of automating education and some social consequences which might result from this automation.

The notion of computer-assisted learning (CAL) has been around for a long time but it is only with the advent of low-cost microcomputers that CAL becomes an economic alternative to conventional classroom teaching.

The principles on which CAL is based are straightforward. The teacher prepares a set of questions and their associated answers. These questions and answers are input to a computer equipped with a CAL program. This program then presents the questions to the student who types his own answers in response. The student's answers are compared, by the computer, with the prepared answers. If his or her answer is wrong, the student is given the opportunity of trying again or, perhaps, revising an earlier part of the course. If the student replies correctly, he or she then moves on to the next, more advanced part of the course.

The advantages of such a system are clear. Students can work at their own speed rather than at the speed dictated by the teacher. Accurate records of each students progress can be maintained by the computer and, once a CAL course is prepared, it can be used by any number of students without incurring additional costs.

Well-designed lessons can be very stimulating indeed. As well as using text output, they can make use of picture and sound output facilities which are now available on many microcomputers. This means that questions can be spoken rather than typed on a screen, the student can point at answers rather than having to type replies, diagrams can be drawn to assist in understanding, and younger children can be encouraged to use the system by rewarding the correct answer with music and pictures.

Students soon become bored with answering a series of questions or reading material off a screen and well-designed CAL lessons must actively involve the student in interesting activities. Probably the best way to do this is to try and make parts of the lesson look like a computer game but this is not easy for many topics.

However, there are also disadvantages associated with CAL. One of these is the difficulty of designing lessons so that they can cope with completely unexpected responses. These unexpected responses may, in fact, be quite logical or may be complete nonsense. The computer can only treat them in the same way whereas a human can discern when a response is based on the misunderstanding of a method and when it is based on the misapplication of a method.

This can be illustrated by example. Say a student is given the simple subtraction problem 327 - 218 and replies with an answer of 111. The logic of this is that the student has subtracted the lower digit from the higher in each place regardless of which number the digit appears. Such an answer indicates that the student does not properly understand subtraction. An answer of 119, on the other hand, probably means that the method was misapplied with a borrow from the ten's place being forgotten.

Another limitation of CAL systems is that they can only be used in the teaching of subjects where the answers to the prepared questions are either definitely wrong or clearly correct. CAL systems cannot really be used to question students on history, language appreciation, etc. where there is no definitive answer to questions but where essay-type answers contain subtle pointers to the student's ability and understanding.

Because of these limitations, it is very unlikely that CAL systems will completely replace teachers in schools. Rather, they will be used to supplement conventional teaching where some material will be presented by the teacher and learning reinforced by the CAL system. When used under supervision, CAL systems can immediately call for help from the teacher when it seems that the student user has some kind of problem.

Some kinds of teaching can be readily supplemented by CAL systems. For example, in science teaching, conventional question/answer CAL systems can be enhanced with facilities to simulate some kinds of experiment and to display experimental results in a clear and understandable way. This means that the student can use the computer to carry out the experiment, prepare his or her results and then go on to work on lessons which are related to that experiment. Some of these experiments will be simulations of common laboratory experiments but the great advantage of simulated experiments is that processes which are normally too complex to ·be carried out in teaching laboratories can be demonstrated to the students.

The advantages of simulated science experiments is that they generally always work and they do not require expensive equipment which is used for that experiment alone. There is not, however, the fun and associated learning involved in setting up experimental apparatus and of having experiments go drastically wrong. Simulated experiments, therefore, supplement rather than replace real experiments.

Another important role for CAL will be in adult education where regular retraining will became part of many jobs. CAL systems are quite suitable for teaching about some new technologies and have the great advantage that they can be used at the convenience of the student. It is likely that some of this retraining will be carried out at special retraining centres equipped with CAL systems and staffed by a small number of trained teachers. Adults will be able to make use of these centres in the evening or at their own convenience and will work at their own speed through the CAL lessons.

In fact, computer-assisted learning is more suited to adult education than it is to the education of young people. Adults taking further education courses are likely to be highly motivated to complete these courses because they understand the benefits of education. The problem of lesson design is less acute as motivated adults do not need constant stimulation to retain their interest in the work.

There will also be a market for leisure-oriented CAL systems to be used in conjunction with home computers and video equipment. These will teach people how to improve their performance at games such as chess and backgammon, how to identify birds, wild flowers, etc. and perhaps they might even instruct in practical tasks such as car maintenance and woodwork. These systems will use a computer integrated with a video disk system which will store pictures of different types of bird, the steps involved in repairing a car's suspension, etc.

A feature of CAL systems, in future, will be their use of computer generated graphics, audio output and unconventional input devices to provide a stimulating learning environment. They will recognise the importance of audio-visual techniques in learning and may even be interfaced to cable television systems allowing access to a vast library of audio-visual material. This leads us on to another important use of information technology in education - the use of educational television (ETV) and teletext systems.

The value of television as an educational medium has been recognised since television transmission began. As well as programmes produced by specialised educational television production units in universities and colleges, some national TV stations also make specific educational programmes. Moreover, general-interest documentaries are of educational value. In the UK, the Open University offers university-level education to part time students all over the country and makes use of television for much of its distance learning.

Three notable advantages of educational television can be identified:

(1)   Television can show dynamic processes such as a robot assembling a component or a computer being used to modify text. These are very difficult to demonstrate in a classroom.

(2)   Cameras can go to places which are physically un-reachable by students, enter dangerous environ-ments and display processes which are not normal-ly visible.

(3)   Activities can be illustrated as they take place in a real environment rather than the simulated environment of the classroom or teaching labora-tory.

There are, of course, some disadvantages with ETV. It is not easy to repeat parts of television programmes or to skip through programmes searching for items of interest. In addition, whilst television is an excellent way of showing what a system can do it is not particularly effective in describing the background to how a system works. For example, it can show the steps involved in using an automated banking system but is not ideal for describing the details of how the system is programmed.

These problems, along with expensive production costs, have restricted the use of ETV. Educational television programmes have tended to be general interest documentaries on topics such as geography or general science. It has been too expensive to make programmes concerned with a single specialised or detailed topic. However, there are three factors likely to change this situation in future:

(1)   The costs of television production equipment are falling as VLSI is used to simplify the electronic circuitry in this equipment.

(2)   Video tape recorders allow programmes to be recorded and played back at the convenience of the student. They allow parts of a programme to be repeated any number of times and the user can even skip through a tape looking for relevant material. Furthermore, it may soon be possible to buy educational TV programmes recorded on video disks. Using these disks, parts of the programme can be located and displayed very quickly indeed. It is possible to combine a video disk system with a CAL system so that the screen display depends on the student's responses to questions posed by the system.

(3)   Cable television allows specialised material to be prepared and broadcast and, ultimately, it may be possible to call up computer-controlled programme libraries for the programme of your choice.

These factors alone mean that more and more ETV programmes will be produced and used in education. However, there is another, more significant factor which will mean that television will come to play a dominant role in some areas of education. This factor is teletext.

We have already seen that teletext systems allow text to be displayed on a TV screen and that it is a straightforward matter to switch between teletext and normal TV transmission. This means that the makers of ETV programmes can supplement pictures of an activity with text explaining the background to what is being seen by the viewer.

For example, an ETV programme on geography might be concerned with the formation of deserts and the film could illustrate desert features such as dunes, oases, etc. The backup text could discuss changing rainfall patterns and describe how deserts are formed. It may even be possible to broadcast, on teletext, computer programs which simulate world rainfall. These can be executed on a home computer so that the viewer can see how apparently small climatic variations can cause deserts to form.

It is almost certain that the developments described here will become widely used in future. Without automation, the education system will not be able to cope with the demands placed on it over the next few years as more and more people demand retraining and leisure education. The need for courses in information technology alone is vast and cannot be met by existing staff simply because too few of them have, themselves, training in this field. Education authorities cannot afford the vast sums needed to retrain existing teachers and there are not enough new teachers around with the necessary background. Although the initial costs of CAL and ETV systems are high, they are much less than the costs of trying to meet this demand for education by conventional means. The automation of education is inevitable.

In the short term, it is probable that many teachers will resist this automation as it will appear that they are being deskilled and replaced by hybrid computer/television systems. To some extent, this is true. Rather than increase the overall number of teachers to cope with increased educational demand, education authorities are more likely to invest in educational technology. There are two principal reasons for this:

(1)   Hiring teachers involves a long-term financial commitment to paying their salaries. Buying equipment, on the other hand, a one-off capital cost followed by relatively small continuing costs for maintenance. In short, computers are cheaper than people!

(2)   Few teachers are equipped to teach information technology as the subject didn't really exist when they were in training. Teachers have neither background nor experience in the subject and retraining them is very expensive indeed.

Of course, educational systems based on information technology will never completely replace teachers. Such systems complement the abilities of the trained teacher and in future, they will become an everyday educational tool. However, they must be used with care as the universal use of information technology in education does have associated disadvantages.

One disadvantage of automated education is that it lacks diversity so that all students receive the same programmes and all are educated into the same way of thinking. This problem is particularly acute in distance-learning programmes where the students do not have ready access to a teacher for help and advice. In situations where all participants think the same way, it is difficult to provoke stimulating discussion and hence to generate new ideas.

A more sinister aspect of the same educational programmes being given to thousands of students is that their entire education could be under the control of relatively few people. Effectively, these few technological educationalists can control the thinking of large segments of the population, suppress ideas with which they do not agree and indoctrinate students into their own way of thought.

A logical consequence of decreased government spending on education and a home-centred life is that there will be moves towards education at home rather than at school. If education is mostly carried out using computers and ETV and teachers can communicate by computer with their pupils, this will certainly be technically possible in the fairly near future.

Although technically possible, it is unlikely that children's education will be organised in this way. Firstly, there are real problems in motivating young children to work when they have no direct contact with their peers and secondly, much of the education which children receive at school actually takes place outside the classroom rather than in a formal teacher/pupil situation. Furthermore, existing houses are not really geared to turning one room into a classroom, and working in cramped conditions with other children present is not particularly conducive to learning.

Finally, dependence on technology is liable to exacerbate the existing educational problems of students who have deprived home backgrounds. Whilst relatively affluent families will be able to afford home computers, extra television sets, video recorders, etc. so that the student can continue his or her schoolwork at home, poor families will not have such luxuries. It will be even more difficult than it is now for their children to progress educationally. This is a social rather than a technological problem and without drastic social changes, it seems that there is little that can be done about it.

3.4   SUMMARY

The fall in the price of electronic components means that it is now possible for homes and schools to afford their own computers. Furthermore, computers will become an integral part of all sorts of domestic appliances such as washing machines and cookers. This chapter has covered the uses of computers in the home and in education.

Many people now have their own personal computer at home. Most use it for playing electronic games but here is an increasingly large number of computer hobbyists. They enjoy devising computer programs and often invent complex and sophisticated programs to automate their everyday tasks. However, it is arguable if it is worth automating household tasks - the most important role of personal computers is recreational.

Computers in the home, built into other equipment, will become pervasive. This chapter has looked at two general applications of microprocessors built into household devices. These applications are in providing

information about the state of a device and in
controlling the operation of the machine. The use of
computers for these functions means that control can be
very precise and that up-to-date information is always
available to the user of the machine.

As computers are used more and more in society,
there is a pressing need for education in computing.
This is discussed in the third section of this chapter.
Devising educational programmes in computing is
difficult and one problem with existing programmes is
that they tend to concentrate on computer programming.
This is a mistake as most people never need to
programme. A well designed course in computing should
concentrate more on the applications and implications
of these machines rather than on their workings.

The need for education in computing and the lack of
trained teachers means that computers themselves must
be used to provide this education. The use of
computers will also affect the teaching of many other
subjects. When combined with educational television
and teletext systems, they offer a powerful new tool to
the educationalist.

This chapter has also looked at a few of the social
implications of computerising the home and education.
By using computers for mail order, education, etc. the
need to leave the home will be reduced. This may mean
an increase in social isolation. Furthermore,
dependence on educational technology and the
standardisation of educational programmes could result
in a decline in creativity and an increase in central
control over education. Rather than being exposed to
all sorts of different ideas from teachers, students
will all follow the same programme and this may lead to
a stifling of initiative.

Chapter 4
The automated workplace

The term 'automation' can be loosely defined to mean the use of machinery to save mental and manual labour. As such, it has been a feature of industrial development over the last two hundred years. Inventions such as the spinning jenny, the steam engine, and the electric motor, which were catalysts of the Industrial Revolution, were means of automating and enhancing muscle power. This automation resulted in immense improvements in labour productivity.

The inventions of the industrial revolution and those that followed certainly did not eliminate the need for human workers. On the contrary, because of increasing markets and growth based on cheap raw materials, many new jobs were created, operating these new machines and in associated service industries.

The new machinery invented during the Industrial Revolution was principally muscle enhancing. It had no inherent decision-making capability. Although some electro-mechanical control systems were developed, proper decision making controllers could not be built into machines until the invention of the minicomputer in the mid-1960s. Now, with microelectronic systems, the cost of an electronic controller is a small fraction of total machine cost.

In itself, this has important implications for manufacturing industry as it means that some machines can be completely automated and no longer require human operators. More significantly, perhaps, computer technology is now sufficiently developed that manufacturing and commercial services, such as offices and mail, can be automated.

Since the 19th century, these services have consumed an increasing proportion of manufacturing costs. It is now estimated that around 50% of manufacturing costs are service costs. Until now, these have not been susceptible to automation.

We shall look at aspects of automation as applied to office services and to manufacturing itself in this chapter. We shall see how computer systems which are built into working tools such as typewriters, telephones, welding machines, etc. will allow a huge increase in labour productivity and reduce manufacturing costs.

Unfortunately, in the context of a world economy which is expanding very slowly, this will almost certainly mean a reduction in the number of job opportunities. Furthermore, not all occupations will be equally affected by this reduction in opportunity. There will still be a need for skilled workers but there will be fewer and fewer unskilled jobs available. The name given to this type of unemployment which directly results from automation is technological unemployment . The final section of this chapter discusses why technological unemployment is an inescapable consequence of automation.

4.1   THE ELECTRONIC OFFICE

It has been estimated that over 60% of the present working population now work in offices and that office costs are the biggest single business expense. This office work is labour rather than capital intensive. In fact, per capita in office equipment is less than 1/10th that of investment in equipment which supports workers directly involved in manufacturing.

These factors mean that the most effective way for business to reduce its costs is to automate its office, using more machines in its office activity. Fewer people need then be employed and running costs are reduced. This has been apparent for some time - LEO, the first commercial computer stood for Lyons Electronic Office - and the widespread use of computers for data processing tasks is a means of reducing office running costs.

In fact, the number of office activities which can be automated by mainframe computers is limited. Whilst the use of these machines has slowed the rate of increase in office costs, they certainly have not curtailed it completely. The reason for this is quite simple - mainframe computers are best suited to repeating the same data processing again and again whereas the majority of office activities are individual activities performed in a relatively unstructured way.

Such activities can only be automated with individual computers which allow different people to carry out different tasks at the same time. The advent of the microprocessor has now made this kind of automation possible. In fact, the fastest growing market for small computers is the office automation market.

Computers have a myriad of uses in offices. They can handle the preparation of text, correspondence, and filing. They can be connected to travel companies computers to simplify business travel bookings. They can act as an electronic diary finding times when groups can meet and reminding office staff of appointments. They can look after all office accounting and bookkeeping.

Only a few of these applications are described here. The topics covered are word processing, office communication systems and office information systems. I shall also discuss some of the changes to office organisation which are sometimes necessary to make the most effective use of information technology.

4.1.1 Word processing

The typing of letters, memos, reports, etc. is undertaken in virtually all offices. Apart from the addition of an electric motor to reduce the work needed to depress the keys, typewriter design has changed little since the first typewriters were introduced in 1874. In modern offices, typewriters are supplemented with photocopying machines which allow multiple copies of a document to be produced from a single typed original.

The fundamental problem with typewritten documents arises if there is a need to modify or add to these documents. Even relatively minor changes such as the addition of a single sentence sometimes means retyping the whole document if the neat appearance of the original is to be maintained. This retyping is uninteresting for the typist and expensive, inasmuch as the cost of adding a single sentence to a document might be the same as the original document production cost.

A word processing system is, in essence, a typewriter which incorporates a computer along with some form of permanent memory device such as a floppy disk. Rather than documents being typed directly onto paper, they are typed into the word processor and displayed on a television-like screen. The typist need not worry about how the document is to be formatted or laid out but can type lines of any length at all. The word processor system subsequently lays out the text neatly as the document is printed. Once input, the document is retained in the computer's memory and may be automatically printed on a high-speed printer any number of times.

There are two major benefits which arise from using a word processor for document preparation. Firstly, the documents are printed in a neat and consistent format with both margins left and right justified, headings automatically centred, pages numbered, etc. Secondly, when document changes are necessary, the copy of the document held in the computer's memory is edited. The required modifications are made and the whole document may be automatically reprinted without unnecessary retyping.

The most common type of editor used with contemporary word processor systems is a screen editor.

The text in the document is displayed on the typists
terminal and corrections are made by overtyping the old
text on the screen. Such editors also include
facilities to delete text and to make space for
additional text to be inserted. It is usually possible
to move text around in the document so that paragraphs
may be rearranged with little effort.

The principle on which screen editors are based is
straightforward. The controlling computer knows the
size of its display screen and can maintain a
correspondence between the text on the screen and the
actual text in the document which is held in its
memory. When changes are made to the text on the
screen, they are reflected in the corresponding text in
the computer's memory.

There are different ways of handling text
insertions, deletions, and the moving of text from
place to place. The most commonly used technique
associates a line number with every line of text and
maintains a list of these line numbers (not necessarily
in sequential order) showing the actual ordering of the
lines displayed on the user's screen. When an editing
session is finished, the document copy in memory is
reorganised by the computer into the order specified in
the line number list. Any deletions, insertions or
changes made by the user are included directly in this
reordered text.

This technique is best illustrated by example. Say
the original text, before editing is:

    There are different ways of handling text (100)
    insertions and deletions.   (200)
    The same techniques are used for text shuffling.
    (300)
   .The most commonly used technique involves storing a
    line number (400)
    with each line of text in memory (500)
    and maintaining a list of line numbers (600)
    showing the actual organisation of the document.
    (700)

The numbers in brackets after each line are the line
numbers allocated to that line by the computer. These
are stored internally and are not displayed on the
user's screen. In its original form, the order of
display of the above text is:

    100 200 300 400 500 600 700

The intention is to transform this text to the first
two sentences of the paragraph immediately preceding
this example so editing operations are required. To
edit the first sentence, line 200 must be changed, line
300 removed and replaced by 'and the moving of text

from place to place. We actually add this text as a completely new line (800). As the changes to line 200 do not involve making that line longer, they are made in place so line 200 becomes:

insertions, deletions, (200)

The display list showing the new sentence replaces line 300 with 800 so after the first set of changes is:

100 200 800 400 500 600 700

The modifications to the second sentence involve adding new text and drastically changing lines 400 to 700. Because these lines have to be made longer, it is not possible to overwrite the text in the computer's memory. Lines are held in sequence in the computer's memory with only a marker showing the end of each line. If a line were to be lengthened this would overwrite the beginning of the following line and information would be lost. New versions of these lines are added to the end of the document and allocated new line numbers.

The most commonly used technique associates a line number (900)
with every line of text and maintains (1000)
a list of these line numbers (not necessarily in sequential order) (1100)
showing the actual ordering of the lines (1200)
to be displayed on the user's screen. (1300).

After these modifications, the revised line display list is:

100 200 800 900 1000 1100 1200 1300

This method of handling document reorganisation works successfully because the way in which the text is displayed and formatted does not depend, in any way, on how that text is stored by the computer. Rather, separate programs exist to display and format text. These ignore the internal organisation and reorganise the text before display or printing.

Because the output produced by a word processor system is so neat, it is actually possible to eliminate the typesetting stage if the final version of a document is to be printed. For example, the text of this book was prepared on a word processor and so-called camera-ready copy was output for subsequent printing. All the text formatting was done by machine and, as this was previously an expensive, labour-intensive operation, its elimination clearly results in cost savings.

When used on their own, word processor systems

improve the quality of documents and, in some situations, allow considerable savings to be made in the costs of document production. However, if an office's major work is producing 'one-off' documents which rarely need revision the use of a word processor will not necessarily reduce typing costs.

The real potential of the word processor results from the fact that it is really a computer rather than a typewriter. As such, it can communicate with other computers. In almost all environments enormous benefits can ensue if word processors are connected together in a communications network.

4.1.2 Electronic mail

At the moment, there are two principal methods of office-to-office communication - by letter and by telephone. These systems work both within an organisation and between different organisations and both suffer from well-known drawbacks.

Letter post is relatively slow and expensive because of its labour intensive nature. Telephone systems do not allow permanent copies of messages to be retained and have the further disadvantage that if a telephone is unanswered for some reason, the message does not get through. It has been estimated that only 15% of business telephone calls are successful in reaching the intended person the first time that they are made.

Telex systems which involve sending hard-copy information along a communication line get round some of these problems but telex is slow, and requires an organisation to be set up to send and receive telex messages. It is, however, the precursor of electronic mail systems which combine the best features of letter post and telephone communication. Ultimately, electronic mail may replace letter post completely for business communications and may drastically reduce the total number of telephone calls which are made.

The distinction between electronic mail and telex is that, in an electronic mail system, the sender of the message does not make a direct connection to the receiver. Rather, he 'posts' his message into the system. The sorting and forwarding of mail is handled automatically by a computer. Electronic mail combines the instantaneous delivery of a telephone call with the guaranteed delivery of a letter.

In an electronic mail system, a message is prepared on a word processor or computer terminal. This message is then entered into a communications network along with the address or addresses of the recipients of the message. The message is sorted by an electronic mail sorter program then dispatched to be received on the recipient's computer. From there, it may be stored, displayed on the recipient's terminal or printed on a high-speed machine.

If the recipient of the message is not using his or her terminal or is too busy to bother with incoming mail the message, unlike a telephone call, is still delivered. It is stored on the recipient's computer and he or she may examine incoming mail whenever time permits. Furthermore, he or she can instruct the computer to automatically acknowledge messages or to dispatch copies of incoming or outgoing mail to other users of the electronic mail system.

At the time of writing, some experimental electronic mail services have been set up which make use of the telephone network for message communication. However, a comprehensive electronic mail system really requires the establishment of new communication networks both nationally and within office buildings themselves.

The existing telephone network in most countries is not really adequate to handle large volumes of electronic mail particularly on the busy inter-city routes. However, the telephone system is being rewired and modernised almost everywhere with low-capacity copper cable being replaced by high-capacity cabling. This process is likely to be complete by the early 1990s and only then will national electronic mail systems come into widespread use.

However, long before then, intra-organisation electronic mail will be well developed. In fact, for large organisations, internal mail represents well over half of the total mail which is generated so the automation of this will result in immediate cost savings. Some companies have already implemented their own electronic mail service but again this is often restricted by the fact that it relies on the internal telephone system.

Now a new type of internal communications network is available which can replace the existing telephone system, carry all computer to computer communications and handle electronic mail.

Existing telephone networks usually have a star pattern with each telephone connected to a central exchange and with all calls switched through that exchange. This is shown in Figure 4.1.

There are a number of disadvantages inherent in this star patterned network:

(1)   The number of lines on the network is limited by the total number of lines which can be handled by the exchange.

(2)   The nature of the system is such that anything apart from two-way connections are difficult to implement.

(3)   Should the exchange break down, the whole system is put out of action.

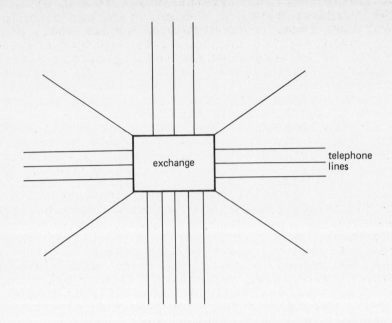

Fig. 4.1   A star telephone network

An alternative organisation which is used by most of
the new internal communications systems (sometimes
called local area networks is to connect all offices
with a ring of cable and to transmit messages on this
ring. This is shown in Figure 4.2.

Messages on the ring are tagged with the address of
both the sender and the receiver and a microprocessor-
based unit in each office examines every message as it
passes by. If the message is intended for that office,
it is collected from the ring otherwise it is simply
sent on its way. If a particular connector finds that
a passing message was actually sent by itself, it then
knows that it has not been delivered (otherwise it
would have been collected). The sender's terminal may
then either cancel the message or try again.

With such a system, there is virtually no practical
limit to the number of ring connections which can be
made, the same message may be broadcast to any number
of destinations and the failure of any one connector
does not affect the operation of the rest of the ring.

Ring systems work well because the ring cable has a
high capacity and a large amount of information can be
transmitted very quickly. Furthermore, each ring
connector splits outgoing messages into packets of
information which are transmitted one-by-one rather
than transmitting the entire message at one time. A
packet of information is simply a group of binary

digits and its interpretation depends on the form of the original message. It may be electronic mail in character form, voice signals which have been converted to binary digits, or input from a sensor device which is being transmitted to another computer.

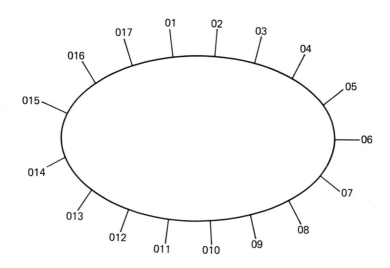

Fig. 4.2   A ring communications network

The receiving ring connector re-assembles the original message from the different packets of information which it has picked up. Because the system can handle tens of thousands of packets per second, the delays involved in this message splitting and re-assembling are not apparent to the user.

Therefore, all office communications whether they be electronic mail, telephone conversations or video images can be handled in the same way. Just as offices now have electrical sockets giving access to mains electricity, in future they will all be equipped with data sockets which will allow devices to be plugged into the local data network.

As well as electronic mail, the availability of a local area network connecting the word processors and computers in an organisation opens up further opportunities for office automation. For example, one of the ring connections might be with a computer controlled photocopying machine. Documents to be duplicated would be transmitted to that machine directly from the word processor where they were prepared without any intermediate handling. Another possibility is to connect a computer with billions of characters of permanent memory to the network and to send all prepared documents to that machine for filing.

4.1.3 Office information systems

The normal office practice for information storage and retrieval is for each office to retain a copy of documents which it produces. These are stored in some kind of filing cabinets. Other copies of the same document may be filed in other departments so that throughout an organisation, there may be several copies of the same document held in different files.

There are two problems which arise from this. Firstly, the physical space required to store these documents is not cheap. It is wasteful to fill much of that space with duplicate documents. Secondly, should the original document be modified at its source, each copy of that document must be traced and replaced by the modified version. This means that a careful record must be kept of who has copies of each document. This is difficult in practice as some people may make copies of copies so that the office which produced the document in the first place may not necessarily have a complete list of recipients.

These problems arise because multiple copies of documents are maintained. They are inherent in any kind of system where several copies of documents may be stored. However, manual filing systems have limitations apart from this and apart from the fact that they take up lots of space. These limitations are due to the fact that once a document has been filed under a particular heading, it can only be retrieved under that heading. Cross referencing without maintaining multiple document copies is difficult. Furthermore, there is no way of initiating document retrieval based on document contents. It is practically very difficult in a large manual filing system to retrieve all documents which somewhere use a particular term such as 'office information system'.

All the problems described above can be circumvented if documents are stored as electronic images on a computer system rather than as paper in a filing cabinet. We have already seen, in Chapter 2, how data base systems can store large amounts of information and can make this readily accessible by creating indexes to the information stored in the system.

If a data base is centrally located and accessible, via a local communications network, a single copy of all the documents produced by an organisation can be stored there. With such a system, cross-referencing is straightforward - a document may appear in several different indexes and, if necessary, the data base management system can perform a context search to find all documents containing particular words or phrases as specified by the user.

Because only a single copy of each document is maintained, the document update problem described above is eliminated. When a document needs to be changed, the original is copied, and changes made. It is then refiled so that the modified document replaces the original. Subsequent access to that document will always find the most up-to-date version.

Centralised information stores for business documents have already been implemented in research laboratories. By 1990, they are likely to be a common feature of many automated offices. All documents produced by an organisation's word processing equipment will be stored there.

This does not mean, however, that manual filing systems will instantly disappear even in organisations which use centralised information storage and retrieval. Apart from the gigantic amount of existing information which must be stored, much of the information in a filing system is generated externally and sent to that office. Until electronic mail becomes universal, this information will come in as paper and will have to be stored in a manual filing system.

For a while, manual and electronic filing systems will co-exist but the advantage of electronic storage are such that, ultimately, all information held on manual systems will be represented and stored electronically. New storage technologies based on video disks are presently under development. These promise vast storage capacities in an area the size of an long playing record. It is estimated that video disks will be able to store 5 billion characters of information in a unit about the size of a large book. By way of comparison, this book contains approximately 350 000 characters so such a system would be able to store the equivalent of around 15 000 books like this.

Existing and incoming paper documents will not have to be retyped to convert them to electronic form. Rather, a computerised scanning machine will scan each page and digitise the image of that page so that it may be stored electronically. Such scanning systems already exist and although they are fairly slow at the moment, it is only a matter of time until fast automatic document readers are available.

4.1.4 Reorganising for automation

It has already been suggested that one reason why automation in offices has been slow to develop is because office tasks are varied and unstructured. Although individual computer systems can handle some of this work, there is no doubt that some office activities are not really amenable to automation. Therefore, to make the most cost-effective use of office automation equipment often involves factoring out activities which can be automated and dedicating people and equipment to these particular tasks.

What this means in practice is that rather than managers having their own personal secretary or administrative assistant, a centralised pool of office support staff must be created to support managerial activities. Some of these staff will be exclusively responsible for using electronic equipment, such as word processors or document scanners, whereas others will be responsible for looking after activities, such as arranging appointments and business trips. These are activities which cannot readily be automated.

As far as the people who work in an office are concerned, the consequences of such a re-organisation are not necessarily beneficial although overall business efficiency may be improved. Rather than having a variety of tasks, office support staff may have to perform a single activity all the time. This is inevitably less interesting and satisfying that a more varied job. Furthermore, personal secretaries are very much status symbols for managerial staff and many managers will not take kindly to having to make use of relatively impersonal centralised facilities.

This exemplifies one of the dilemmas of automation. When computer systems are introduced as tools, making the most of them often involves changing long-established practices. There seem to be no real, sensible alternative to making these changes but they must be introduced through consultation with the individuals involved and in such a way that individual job satisfaction is maintained.

4.2   AUTOMATED MANUFACTURING

Automated manufacturing really started around the beginning of the 19th century with the introduction of powered machinery. These machines were designed and introduced throughout that century and their activities become more and more interrelated. This mutual dependence of one machine on another came to its logical culmination with the assembly line introduced by Henry Ford at the beginning of this century.

As I have already said in the introduction to this chapter, the role of this machinery was to enhance the muscle power of workers and machines still required a human operator to make decisions on how to control that machine. The tools on the machines were driven by motors and the job of the operator was to guide these tools over the workpiece. In many jobs, exactly the same sequence of control actions were repeated again and again by the machine operator.

One of the problems of human control of a repetitive process is that inevitably there will be small differences in each repetition of the process. In most cases, these are unimportant but sometimes small flaws in different components can eventually result in the final product being sub-standard. Accordingly, a system of quality control is necessary to check production quality and to reject sub-standard products.

One of the principal advantages of automating the control of repetitive processes is that greater production consistency is achieved. The machine can repeat the process again and again without variation. Such control automation was first introduced about 30 years ago with so-called numerically controlled (n.c.) machines. These incorporated simple control logic and a control program on paper tape governed the operations of the machine.

The widespread introduction of n.c. machines in the 1950s prompted suggestions that, within a few years, manufacturing would be totally automated with only a few white-coated technicians needed to look after the n.c. machines. These suggestions were quite unrealistic for a number of reasons:

(1)   In order for an n.c. machine to switch from one task to another, a completely different paper tape had to be loaded into the machine. This operation took several minutes so there was no way in which n.c. machines could handle several different tasks in quick succession.

(2)   There was little or no automated handling of materials at that time and even now materials handling is one of the most difficult task to automate.

(3)   The n.c. control programs were quite primitive and there was no way in which the machines could be programmed to cope with unexpected events.

(4)   Inter-machine communications were more or less non-existent so that the actions of different machines could not readily be co-ordinated.

Since the introduction of n.c. machines, automatic machine control has been steadily refined. Modern n.c. machines incorporate a mini or micro computer and can switch programs very quickly indeed. They may also be multi-functional and not necessarily dedicated to a single task. Programming techniques have also improved and complex control programs can now be implemented. It is now also possible to coordinate the activities of all machines by connecting all of them to a central computer. This machine can also act as a fault finder detecting when a component has failed. Although the completely automated factory is not yet a reality, it is certainly in sight for some kinds of manufacturing. The dream of the 1950s, automated factories run by technicians, will be the reality of the 21st century.

4.2.1 Computer-aided design

In preparing the design of a product, the engineering designer must take a variety of factors into account:

(1)   He must design an object which meets its specification.

(2)   He must take the styling and exterior appearance into account - the product should be good to look at.

(3)   He must optimise the use of materials by making use of the minimum amount of the cheapest possible material without compromising the strength and durability of the finished product.

(4)   He must optimise the use of tools and labour by designing a product which can be manufactured at minimum cost.

The designer uses his knowledge and experience to trade off these factors in producing the final design. This final design is expressed as a drawing or blueprint which can be read and understood by those responsible for manufacturing the product.

Manual design is very time consuming. The designer must consult books of tables giving the characteristics of materials, must perform a large number of calculations and must carefully draw his finished design. This drawing takes a lot of time yet the drawings themselves are often made up of repetitive elements. Having drawn the first element, the designer is no longer carrying out creative work.

Because of the time required for manual design, it is often impossible to optimise the use of tools and materials so that finished products are sometimes unnecessarily expensive and limited in performance.

Computer-aided design (CAD) was one of the early applications of computers but those early CAD systems were limited to helping the engineer with the calculations needed for his design. These systems have now become much more sophisticated and incorporate computer graphics systems, automated design checking, etc.

A modern computer-aided design system such as that shown in Figure 4.3 can take over almost all the repetitive aspects of engineering design. Present day computer-aided design systems are equipped with very powerful graphics capabilities. The engineer can input his drawing directly into the system using a special drawing board called a graphics tablet. Alternatively, he or she can produce a rough drawing on paper and have this read by a scanner which digitises the drawing and passes the digital image to the computer.

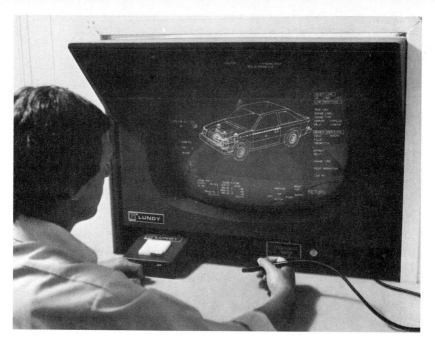

Fig. 4.3   A computer-aided design system

Once input, the drawing can be automatically tidied up, rotated, expanded, contracted and displayed as a 2 or 3 dimensional model. Given one drawing, the system can repeat it any number of times either directly or as a mirror image. Repetitive elements need only be drawn once and, if the design is symmetric, only one half need be drawn by the designer. This is then automatically mirrored by the CAD system to create the complete drawing.

With such a CAD systems, drawings which were previously uneconomic to produce such as an 'exploded' view of the components of a machine, can be automatically generated. The CAD system can directly reduce manufacturing costs and improve performance by optimising the use of materials, tools and labour. As an illustration of this, a Boeing engineer reckoned that had the BAC1-11, a manually designed British airliner, been designed with Boeing's CAD system, it would have been at least a ton lighter. This would have meant consequent improvements in load carrying, range, fuel consumption, etc. and, perhaps, the commercial success of the aircraft.

The existence of CAD systems allows some completely new designs to be created which could not possibly be designed manually. The best example of this is VLSI design which is almost completely based on CAD systems for graphics, circuit simulation, and design verification.

Some CAD systems now include facilities for automatically generating programs for computer controlled machine tools. These give instructions to the tool how to implement the design. The ultimate aim is to devise a computer system which combines design and manufacturing automation. This computer-aided design/computer-aided manufacturing system would handle a product from its initial stages of design through to completed production.

4.2.2 Industrial robotics
The popular image of a robot, fostered by science fiction writers, is that of a highly intelligent metal man. The robot may be endearing, frightening, or immensely powerful but in all cases it has super-human abilities and intelligence. The reality is much more mundane. In fact, the word 'robot' is derived from the Czech word for worker and this is a very apt description of a modern industrial robot. Figure 4.4 is a photograph of a typical robot, acting as a welder.

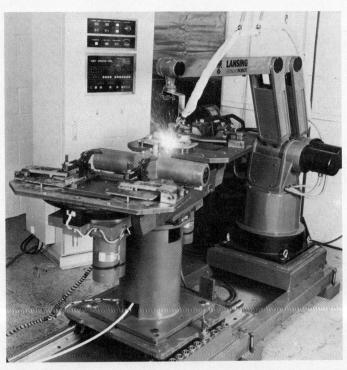

Fig. 4.4   A typical industrial robot

Today's industrial robots really consist of an arm on a trunk. The arm may be jointed at the elbow and wrist and may be able to swivel and move in and out from the shoulder. It has an associated computer control and a hand which acts as a tool holder. This holder can be fitted with a number of different types of tool such as a welding torch, a paint spray, or a gripper of some kind.

This universal tool holder and the number of degrees of freedom of the robot's arm movement constitute the important differences between a robot and other computer-controlled machinery. Where other computer-controlled machines are uni-functional - they can only carry out a single task such as drilling, welding, cutting, painting, etc. - robots are multi-functional. The same basic robot can be used for a variety of different tasks - materials handling, painting, welding or all sorts of other jobs.

Robots are used for some kinds of assembly work but, as described below, present-day robots are not well-suited to this kind of task. As a result, the most common applications of robots is welding, spray painting and the moving of hot, heavy and dirty objects from place to place.

A feature of the present generation of industrial robots is their ability to switch, very quickly, from one program to another. Other computer-controlled machines often cannot switch as quickly because as well as program switching, they must also be reset and realigned for the new work. The robot's flexibility allows this resetting to be automatic.

This ability to switch from one control program to another without human intervention means that robots can be used in small batch production operations. Say a manufacturer makes a number of variants of some basic object such as a car body, a bath, or a casing for a TV set. With ordinary n.c. machines, each variant must be made in large batches and the machine reset between each batch. With robots, the machines can switch at will between programs to handle each variant.

The production of each type of object can be adjusted to the market demand with, perhaps, only three or four instances of a particular variant being made. This means that, for little extra cost, many variants of a product can be offered to the buyer.

Although present-day robots are much more flexible than uni-functional machines, they are neither as flexible as humans nor as efficient at a particular task as a machine designed specifically for that task. Furthermore, as with humans, the price paid for mobility and flexibility is that robots cannot be made powerful enough to lift very heavy workpieces. As a result, their usefulness in materials handling is limited to relatively lightweight objects.

The present generation of robots, however, can only blindly follow instructions. In general, they are only equipped with the most primitive sensors to detect the presence or absence of a workpiece and they have no sense of sight or touch. The workpieces on which the robot is operating must be exactly aligned. If not, the robot will act as if its workpiece is in the correct place and carry out its program.

This lack of sensors places constraints on workpiece alignment and production line design. For example, if some part is made up of a few components, the order in which these components are given to a human is irrelevant. He or she can easily recognise each component, sort them out and assemble them in any order which suits themselves.

A robot however must receive the parts in a particular order, must have some way of holding parts in alignment and must carry out the assembly in a predefined sequence. If parts are missing, presented upside down, or out of order the robot cannot cope. It will fail to assemble the required object.

As a result, production lines which make use of robots for assembly work depend on parts sorting devices and, sometimes, humans organising the parts for the robot to assemble. This obviously negates some of the cost advantages of automated production based on robots.

Some of the problems in using robots for assembly work result from the fact that there is not an formal, unambiguous way of describing this work. That is, we don't have a language which can be used for programming robots. Rather, robot programming relies on a technique called teach-and-tell. This technique is comparable to that which might be used to show a small child how to draw the letters of the alphabet where an adult takes the child's hand and traces the shape of the letter required.

For robots, teach-and-tell programming consists of an operator guiding the machine through the sequence of actions for a particular job. He uses a manual control unit to guide the robot hand through space and shows it where to perform manipulations, switch on tools, etc. The machine remembers the path that its hand has taken and the actions to be taken at each point in the path. It can subsequently repeat them indefinitely at high speed.

Of course, the problem with this teach-and-tell technique is that it does not teach the robot anything about the task it is carrying out. The robot has no idea that it is welding, painting, etc. - it only knows where to move its hand and when to switch things on and off. The robot cannot accept instructions such as 'pick up a bolt' but is instructed to perform a picking up action where the operator expects the bolt to be. Using teach-and-tell, there is no way to instruct the robot to do an action only if some condition holds - the action must be carried out regardless of whether its workpiece is set up, its paint supply has run out, or an object is there for it to pick up.

In order to improve the capability of industrial robots, two related developments are required. Firstly, robots must be equipped with sensors so that they can be aware of their environment. Secondly, new programming languages must be developed for instructing robots how to do their job.

Two types of sensor which are likely to be incorporated into the next generation of industrial robots are vision sensors allowing the robot to see its workplace and touch sensors allowing the machine to feel what it is doing.

Vision sensors operate by scanning a scene with television-type cameras and recognising objects in the field of view. Some of the problems of implementing computer vision are discussed in the next chapter - it is a difficult problem to solve. In general, it is impossible to equip robots with a vision capability comparable to that of humans. The best they can do at the moment is to recognise simple outlines against a plain background. However, even this limited capability can dramatically enhance the abilities of robot systems.

For example, if a robot can recognise a component irrespective of the way in which that component lies, this would eliminate much of the need for the pre-sorting of parts. The machine could simply be presented with the components of an object, could select them in the right order, then carry out the assembly. Alternatively, it might be most efficient to use several robots working in parallel - a vision equipped robot to organise the parts and 'blind' robots to do the actual assembly.

When humans are assembling an object, they do not just use their eyesight to align the components of that object. Whilst the gross alignments are carried out by eye, fine alignments are done by touch - we feel that one part fits snugly against another. This use of touch is particularly important when we are assembling small parts with fine tolerances.

The simplest robot touch sensors simply detect whether or not the robot's hand is gripping a part. These are very simple to incorporate in a robot and consist of a switch which closes when the robot's 'fingers' come together. If this switch closes when it is not expected to, this means that nothing has been gripped by the hand.

More complex sensors depend on using compression gauges and delicate springs built into the robot's hand. The gauge measures the compression on the springs which is minimised when an interlocking part slides into place. In Figure 4.5, the springs are compressed as the part does not fit into the hole whereas in

Figure 4.6, the component is properly assembled and the springs on the robot's hand are relaxed. To fit the part, the robot moves it along the flat surface until it slots into place and spring compression is minimised.

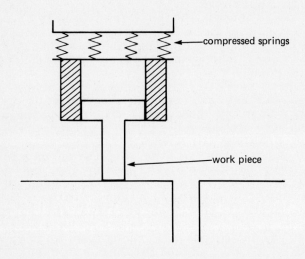

Fig. 4.5   Robot touch sensor – part not fitting

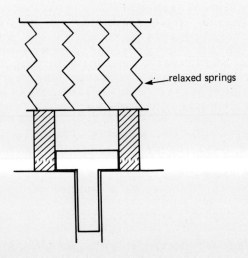

Fig. 4.6   Robot touch sensor – part in place

Touch sensors such as those described above have already been tested successfully in research laboratories. Robots equipped with this sense can assemble complex objects made up of many small parts. It is likely that robots like this, equipped with touch sensors, will be in general use before the end of this decade.

Whilst there is a good deal of research work going on into the design of programming languages for robots, the problem is an extremely difficult one to solve. So-called comprehensive assembly instructions for humans are not comprehensive at all but rely on an enormous amount of built-in knowledge which humans have. Such knowledge is not inherent in robots so the machine does not know, for instance, that the purpose of a bolt is to join pieces of material, that nuts fit on bolts, etc.

This means that robots can't be told what to do in the same way as humans can be given instructions. Realistically, machines which can understand such instructions are not likely to be developed in the near future. Rather robot programming will move from pure 'teach-and-tell' to some hybrid technique involving simple instructions on how to do a task combined with teach-and-tell demonstrations on how to move through space.

Although an extremely important development, robot systems are only one aspect of automated manufacturing. Dedicated computer-controlled machines will become more sophisticated and offer more and more facilities. They will continue to be used in situations where a large volume of work is carried out. Materials handling will be automated so that work will automatically move from machine to machine and computerised fault diagnosis systems will be introduced to check the functioning of these automated systems.

In an automated factory, a computer system will be used to design a product and this design will be passed directly to the automated machines on the production line. These will fetch the raw materials required, machine the parts as necessary and them assemble them, all with minimal human intervention. This may seem to be a scenario from a science fiction book but, to a limited extent, such systems already exist in some car plants. By the end of the century they will be a common feature of large-scale manufacturing enterprises.

4.3   TECHNOLOGICAL UNEMPLOYMENT

The effects of automation on the numbers of people employed in government, commerce, and industry have been, by far, the most widely publicised implication of the introduction of information technology. Comments on this have ranged from the optimistic, suggesting that many more employment opportunities will be created by automation, to the pessimistic, which expect only a minority of the population to have a job.

It is unlikely that either of these extremes will result. However, there will be very significant changes in the job market both in the numbers of jobs and the type of work which is available. I believe that there will inevitably be some reduction in employment opportunities because of the influence of information technology. This so called technological unemployment is the topic discussed here.

It is not my intention to try and put figures on the numbers of unemployed in 1990, 2000, or whatever. Rather, I want to look at why such unemployment is inevitable, at least in Western Europe and North America. The social consequences of long-term technological unemployment are not covered here but are discussed in Chapter 8.

The introduction of new technology is only one of many interrelated factors which affect the numbers of jobs available. Some of the most important of the other factors affecting employment opportunities are:

(1)   The costs of energy and raw materials.

(2)   The world economic state - at the time of writing, the world is in the midst of a deep economic depression which has reduced markets in almost all countries of the world.

(3)   The comparative rates of inflation of a country and its competitors.

(4)   Government policy which may have a particular aim such as the reduction of unemployment or the control of inflation.

(5)   The inherent riches of a country such as gold mines, oil wells, mineral deposits, etc.

(6)   The level of education and expectations of a country's workforce.

(7)   The social structure within a country. In some countries, it is normal practice for all members of a family to work together and even though some members of that family may be underemployed, they do not consider themselves to be unemployed. This is particularly true of countries whose economies are based on small family farms.

Because all of these factors and the effects of automation are closely interlinked, it is not possible to pinpoint exactly which jobs are lost because of automation and which losses are due to some other factor such as a depressed economy. It is only possible to look at historical trends and the potential of information technology itself. These suggest that jobs will actually be lost because of automation.

Firstly, automated machinery can take over many jobs which are now done by people. Such machines do not get tired, go on strike, or require breaks. They make fewer mistakes than humans and often do the job better. They can be reprogrammed rather than expensively retrained should the job they do become obsolete. Furthermore, they obviously do not have to be paid although initial costs and maintenance costs may be high.

However, it must also be remembered that they do not recycle money in the economy. Robots don't buy cars! In this respect, productivity increases due to automation are quite different from those in the past. Previously, improved productivity meant more pay for workers and more jobs created. This increased the market for goods so that the increased productivity could be absorbed. Introducing robots does not, in itself, increase the demand for products produced by these robots.

Secondly, integrated electronic components have simplified the design of many products which therefore require fewer people to build them. As an example of this, the Japanese TV industry halved its workforce between 1972 and 1976 yet produced about 10 million sets in 1976 compared to 8 million in 1972. Comparable workforce reductions have been a feature of many other industries where electronic components have replaced mechanical or electro-mechanical assemblies. For instance, the Swiss watch industry was almost completely eliminated by the introduction of electronic digital watches.

Thirdly, simplified manufacturing techniques resulting from integrated components do not necessarily require a well-educated and highly skilled workforce, particularly for routine assembly work. As a result, multinational companies are moving this kind of work to low-wage countries in Asia and South America such as Thailand, India and Brazil. Although this may not be a permanent move, it will have significant short-term employment consequences for North America and Europe. Ultimately, as automated assembly techniques are refined, this assembly work may be moved back to Europe and North America creating unemployment problems in developing countries but without creating many new jobs in the developed world. Some commentators (particularly politicians) accept these facts but continue to maintain that the jobs created in new industries, based on information technology, will outnumber those lost through automation and job exporting. Their justification for this premise is historical. Technological unemployment has resulted from innovations such as the spinning jenny, the steam engine, the motor car, and the tractor but that after a few years enough new jobs have been created for those put out of work.

Up till recently, technological unemployment in the industrialised countries was compensated by an increase in the number of jobs resulting from the new technology. This increase was due to the fact that markets for goods were expanding. The increased production required more labour.

Now, the potential for businesses in Europe and North America expanding their market is limited for the reasons discussed below:

(1)   Industry is no longer solely concentrated in North America and Europe. Countries such as Brazil, Korea, and India are industrialising rapidly and competing for markets which until recently were captive to European and American industry. Furthermore, these new industrial nations have no restraining backlog of existing, obsolete plant nor historically restrictive working practices. They can immediately invest in modern computer-controlled machinery and hence become more efficient than existing industrial nations.

(2)   Previous industrial expansion was undertaken using cheap energy, raw materials, and labour. None of these are now available in 'old' industrialised countries. This means that the unit costs of goods is inevitably fairly high.

(3)   The consumer market in America and Europe is almost completely satisfied. Almost everyone has a television, the majority have cars, telephones, refrigerators, etc. There is little scope for market expansion in these countries yet in countries where their exists a potentially large market for these goods, the people are too poor to afford them. They are unlikely to become significantly richer in future because the development of their industries is hindered by high energy and raw material costs in combination with large foreign debts.

There will certainly be some new jobs created in industries which are based on information technology. There already is an increasing demand for those skilled in electronics and computing. However, these industries are not inherently labour intensive so the numbers of jobs created is unlikely to match the numbers of jobs lost through automation. Furthermore, there will only be a limited increase in the size of the market so that there will not be any need to expand the workforce to cope with increased production demands.

Another factor which makes technological unemployment inevitable is the fact that those put out of work by automation are, in general, unskilled. They cannot just move into jobs associated with information technology. Many of them will not have the educational background for retraining, many will be close to retirement age. None of these people will have access to the jobs created by information technology.

Therefore, an unavoidable consequence of introducing information technology will be a significant increase in the total numbers of unemployed in Europe and North America. This unemployment will mostly affect unskilled workers and those young people leaving school with few or no formal qualifications.

However, if any one country chooses not to modernise its industry, rejects information technology, and maintains existing working practices, it is likely that the employment consequences will be at least as severe. The productivity advantages gained through automation are such that non-automated manufacturing industry will not be able to compete in world markets with their automated counterparts. Non-automated industries will go out of business and their workers will become unemployed. One way or another, then, higher unemployment is inevitable.

I will conclude this chapter with a quote from a book called 'The Collapse of Work', published in 1979 by Methuen. This book is written by two prominent British trade unionists, Clive Jenkins and Barrie Sherman, and it is all about the employment consequences of information technology. This quote refers to the numbers of unemployed in the UK but the principle is universal:

> Remain as we are, reject the new technologies and we face unemployment of up to 5.5 million by the end of the century. Embrace the new technologies, accept the challenge and we end up with unemployment of about 5 million...What is clear is that whichever road we take, work will collapse.

4.4   SUMMARY

This chapter has been concerned with how information technology will affect work. It concentrates on the two areas of work which employ most people - office work and manufacturing - and discusses how information technology will be used in these environments. The chapter also discusses the effects of information technology on employment. It concludes that society must learn to adapt to a situation where full-time employment is not necessarily available for all who want it.

The electronic office is the first topic discussed here. Offices are ripe for automation as they are labour intensive and expensive to run. Many office functions will be automated in the near future. Word processing systems will replace typewriters in many cases, simplifying the task of repetitive text preparation. New office communication systems will be established allowing word processors to communicate. These will provide a basis for electronic mail systems to replace existing letter post. Centralised storage of information where all documents are stored on a central data base will become commonplace.

All of these changes may require existing office organisations to be modified so that office workers have clearly defined functions such as 'word processor operator'. This contrasts with the existing situation where most staff have general duties encompassing a number of distinct functions.

The second major section in this chapter discusses automated manufacturing. It concentrates on two aspects of this - computer-aided design and robots. Computer-aided design systems are intended to simplify the task of the engineering designer by taking over many of the repetitive aspects of his job. They perform calculations, assist with creating blueprints, and perform some checking of the design. Ultimately, such systems may be integrated with computerised manufacturing systems so that the entire production of a product can be automated.

Robots are not the intelligent metal humanoids beloved of science fiction writers but are very unintelligent machines. They differ from other computer controlled machines inasmuch as they are flexible - the same robot can carry out assembly, welding, painting, etc. Essentially robots consist of an arm on a trunk and their flexibility is due to the fact that different tools can be used by the robot's hand. Future generations of robots will be equipped with sensors which will enable them to find out about the environment in which they work. They will have limited senses of sight and touch which will allow them to identify, align, and assemble objects. By the year 2000, we may see completely automated factories with virtually all work carried out by robots.

The automation of the workplace inevitably means that there will be fewer jobs available for people. Automated equipment and tools will allow vast increases in personal productivity. Many fewer people will be needed to attain present production levels. Those displaced by automation will not find new jobs created

by industries based on information technology. One
reason for this is that not that many new jobs will be
created, the other that they are untrained for these
new types of job. Society must learn to adapt to
limited job opportunities.

Chapter 5
Cash and the computer

Over the centuries, the nature of money has changed. Coins made of precious metals like gold and silver have been almost completely replaced by paper notes and when large amounts of money changes hands, these transactions are almost always made by cheque or bank draft. Now, information technology is about to change the nature of money yet again. Cheques will disappear, banknotes will be replaced by cash cards and even the small change in your pocket might become obsolete.

In this chapter, we shall look at existing systems in banking and other financial institutions and see how computers are already being used. We shall then go on to look at developments in these systems and at retail systems where computers are appearing in supermarkets, stores and even the local pub. When retail systems and financial systems communicate directly, the need for paper money (cash and cheques) will disappear. The third part of the chapter looks at how this cashless society might be implemented.

If cash disappears, the criminal's principal motivation is eliminated. As the cashless society is introduced, changing patterns of crime will result. In the final part of the chapter, therefore, we shall look at computers and crime.

5.1   COMPUTERS AND FINANCE

Collectively, the major financial institutions such as banks, insurance companies, etc. are probably the richest and the most powerful force in any non-communist society. They tend to be inherently conservative in their practices, and maintain traditional ways of doing business. However, the implementation of these practices has changed radically with the advent of computer systems. The financial institutions are amongst the largest and most innovative users of computers. Their everyday working is now totally dependent on large and powerful computer systems.

Until the late 1970s, the role of the computer in financial systems was almost entirely confined to data processing, and this is still their major function.

The amount of data which has to be processed by a major bank, for instance, is immense. A bank is likely to have to maintain millions of accounts and process hundreds of thousands of transactions every day. It has to account carefully for a vast number of banknotes, process many cheques and ensure that its depositors' money is wisely invested. It also has to handle foreign exchange transactions, arrange for account holders to be kept up-to-date on the state of their accounts and act as a general financial advisor to its customers.

It is fair to say that providing these services on the scale which is now expected would be quite impossible without sophisticated and complex data processing systems. However, it is not the purpose of this book to discuss computerised data processing. Rather, we shall now look at how the financial institutions are making use of information technology, how this is improving their customer services and how it promises to change these institutions themselves.

5.1.1 Customer services

It is a common complaint that banks are never open when you want them. They close before the end of normal working hours and at weekends, just when large numbers of people want to make use of their services. Although this is irritating, it is understandable - banks have a major bookkeeping task at the end of every working day. If they stayed open after normal working hours, the bank staff would not be able to go home until well into the evening.

To be fair, the banks have always been aware of the problems of customers who must make special arrangements to leave work in order to visit a bank. Until recently, however, there was little they could do to help them. Now, information technology offers an opportunity to provide some banking services, automatically, 24 hours a day, 7 days a week.

These services are provided by a microprocessor controlled terminal such as that shown in Figure 5.1. Such customer-operated terminals are now a common sight outside many banks. They allow customers to withdraw cash, query the state of their accounts, order a new cheque book, and so on.

When using one of these automatic bank tellers, the customer inserts a plastic card into the machine. This card includes a magnetic strip which holds encoded information about the customer's account number. Once the automatic teller has read the account number, it asks for a secret password (usually a four digit number) known only to the owner of the card and the system. This ensures that if the card has been stolen, the thief cannot use it to withdraw cash. Once identified, the customer can them make use of the banking services provided by the system.

Fig. 5.1   An automated teller terminal

The teller terminal works by reading the customer's account number from his card and transmitting that number to the bank's central computer. This machine has details of all accounts. The central computer then informs the terminal of the customer's password which is compared with the password punched in by the terminal user. If they are the same, the transaction continues. If the personal identity code typed by the customer does not match the code known to the computer, the machine requests the code number to be retyped. The customer is allowed to try the code once or twice more in case a genuine mistake has been made. If the codes do not match after two or three tries, the terminal assumes that the card is stolen and that the terminal user is trying to defraud the system. In this case, it ends the dialogue with the customer and does not return the card.

The role of the teller terminal in the transaction is to act as an interface to the customer and to translate his push button requests into internal codes. These are transmitted to and processed by the bank's computer. For example, say a customer wishes to withdraw 20 pounds from his account. He first punches the 'withdraw cash' button, then the amount required.

The terminal repeats this amount to the customer and asks him to verify it by pressing some other key. A code meaning 'withdraw cash', the customer's account number and the amount requiredis then sent to the bank's central computer. This machine checks the customer's account and if he or she has enough money, responds with a code indicating that the transaction can continue.

At the same time, the computer debits the customer's account by the amount of cash withdrawn. When the terminal receives the code from the central computer, it starts an automatic cash counting mechanism to provide the money for the customer.

A clever feature of the terminal's design is that it is not possible for the customer to forget his or her card. Before the cash is actually handed over, the card must be withdrawn from the machine. When an internal sensor detects that the card has been removed, the cash dispenser is activated and the money passed to the customer.

The same card may be used, in some banks, inside the bank in place of the traditional passbook which keeps details of the customer's transactions. Each bank teller is equipped with a special terminal which can read the customer's card. The teller can carry out all of his or her functions using this terminal rather than recording the transaction on paper. Rather than use the traditional technique of recording transactions on special forms which are subsequently processed, the bank teller inputs the customer's card into a special counter terminal. This terminal reads the card and identifies the customer to the bank's computer. Transactions are processed immediately by the computer rather than after the bank has closed for the day.

Computer-controlled banking terminals are still usually installed in or outside bank buildings. In principle, however, there is no reason why such terminals may not be installed in supermarkets, railway stations, factories or any other place.

At the time of writing, some initial experiments towards this are in progress. One supermarket has installed a system which allows cash to be transferred directly from the customer's account to the supermarket's account. The required cash is then handed over to the customer. The feature of this system is that no bank staff are involved - staff employed by the supermarket use a computer controlled terminal to run the system.

Another example of a financial transaction system which is not installed in a bank is a petrol purchasing system which a number of banks are experimenting with. Using this system, the customer pays for petrol by instructing funds to be transferred from his or her account to the service station's account. If the service station is itself self service, such a system could provide a completely automated 24 hour petrol purchasing service.

This example of an automated petrol purchasing system is an instance of a simple form of electronics funds transfer. In this case, the receiver is fixed (the service station) and the sender must use the same bank as the receiver. Processing a transaction involves looking up the sender's account to check that funds are available, debiting the amount by the amount of the sale and immediately crediting that amount to the service station's account. Electronic funds transfer (EFT) is the name given to computerised systems which can automatically debit and credit bank accounts. Thus money can be transferred from buyer to seller without human intervention.

A general purpose EFT system will be much more flexible than the petrol purchasing system. Say customer A wishes to sent money to customer B who does not use the same bank as customer A. A will be able to input a code which identifies B's bank and his account number. The computer will recognise that B is not a customer and will initiate some kind of inter-bank communication system. Once contact with B's bank's computer is made, funds will be debited from A's account and credited to B's. The transaction will take place via an inter-bank communication network.

Of course, a major problem with all of these services is that there is little or no standardisation in the services provided and mechanisms used. This means that, for automated petrol sales say, the service is limited to those customers who use the same bank as the service station. There is no reason why this should be the case. In normal banking practice, cheques of any one bank are handled and processed by all banks. Automated procedures are relatively straightforward and it ought to be possible to establish standards in this field.

As well as improving customer service, all of these automated banking systems will, in the long term, reduce costs and provide the bank with more detailed and up-to-date accounts. Each piece of paper which passes through by the bank whether it be a cheque, an account withdrawal slip, or a banknote costs money inasmuch as that paper must be handled and accounted for. This cost is more or less independent of the amount of the transaction. So, for transactions which involve relatively small amounts, the cost of that transaction is a significant fraction of the amount involved.

These small transactions, typically personal rather than business transactions, are those which are most readily automated. It is reasonable to predict that, in future, the banks will encourage more and more personal banking to be carried out by interacting with a computer system rather than a bank teller.

5.1.2 Inter-bank communication systems

The idea of electronic funds transfer has already been introduced and although such systems are still in their infancy, in future more and more payments will be made by EFT. The basis for EFT systems has existed since the mid-seventies in the sophisticated inter-bank communication systems which have been developed.

In this section, I shall describe present day inter-bank communication and EFT systems, explain their operation, and show how they might be developed into a completely automated system for transferring funds, nationally or internationally, from one bank account to another.

An impressive example of inter-bank communication is the SWIFT system. This is a world-wide, computer controlled, message switching system which allows member banks to communicate rapidly with each other and to pass transaction orders from bank to bank. SWIFT is not an EFT system - funds are not directly transferred via SWIFT messages - but is a fast and efficient electronic mail system allowing banks to exchange missives.

To make use of the SWIFT system, the bank must become a member of SWIFT, which stands for 'Society for Worldwide Financial Transactions'. The bank may then communicate with all other banks who are also members of SWIFT. A message to be sent from one SWIFT member to another is encoded in standard SWIFT format and input to the sending bank's computer. This message includes codes indicating the sender and the receiver as well as the text of the message which is to be sent.

The sending bank's computer then transmits the message to a national message concentrator computer which collects all messages from a particularly country. In effect, this concentrator is a national sorting house for messages which must pass through this system before being forwarded.

This message concentrator is connected via fast data transfer lines to a SWIFT operating centre which is analogous to an international sorting office. The operating centre examines the message, finds the destination and passes the message to that country's SWIFT concentrator. This concentrator looks at the message, identifies the destination bank and passes the message to that bank's computer centre. At the same time, an acknowledgement is sent to the SWIFT operating centre which ultimately reaches the sending bank via its own local concentrator and computer centre.

At the time of writing, the SWIFT system has three operating centres (in Belgium, Holland, and the USA). All messages pass through one of these centres. Each country has one or more concentrators with all member banks in that country connected to that concentrator. This is shown schematically, in Figure 5.2.

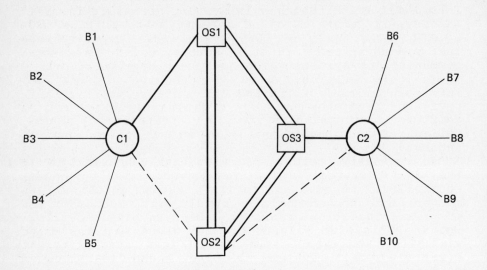

Fig. 5.2   SWIFT network organisation

A message to be sent from B3 to a destination bank B8 say, is switched from B3 to C1 (the local concentrator), then from C1 to OS1 (the operating centre). It is then passed by the operating centre OS1 to OS3, from OS3 to concentrator C2 and, finally from there to B8.

Because of the redundancy built into the SWIFT system, where any part may be bypassed, the system is almost constantly available in spite of computer or communication breakdown.

Each local concentrator is connected to more than one operating centre. The solid line in Figure 5.2 indicates the normal operating centre used by that concentrator, and the broken line, the operating centre which may be used if the first centre is unavailable. Each operating centre is designed so that it can handle the work of another centre as well as its own work should this be necessary because of computer or communication failure. Although not shown on Figure 5.2, the local concentrator may also be bypassed should it fail. Banks may communicate with another country's concentrator using ordinary telephone lines.

The SWIFT system is what is known as a 'store and forward' system where messages are sent to some central computer, stored and then subsequently forwarded to their destination. It is run by an independent organisation and each member bank pays for its usage of the system.

An alternative organisation of a banking communication system is the CHAPS system which is presently being implemented by the major clearing banks in the UK. CHAPS stands for Clearing House Automated Payments System and will handle national inter-bank communications while SWIFT handles international transactions. In the CHAPS system, bank computers will communicate directly rather than through an intermediary. It is more like a telephone system rather than a mail system. By using CHAPS, much of the present paperwork involved in inter-bank transactions will be eliminated.

These communication systems, when integrated with automated customer services, will allow completely automated electronic funds transfer to be implemented. The customer will be able to transfer money directly from account to account without any paperwork whatsoever.

5.2   COMPUTERISED SHOPPING

Until very recently, computers in shops had a limited role. Large stores and supermarkets made use of computers for traditional data processing functions - accounting, payroll, stock control, etc. but, as far as the shopper was concerned, these were completely invisible functions. Now, microelectronics means that it is worthwhile introducing computer systems into the shop itself.

This change is most obvious in large department stores and supermarkets which are introducing so-called point-of-sale terminals. Electronic point-of-sale terminals (EPOS terminals) are microprocessor controlled terminals which combine the functions of a cash register and a computer terminal. They work as a cash register but also exchange information about the goods being purchased with a central computer somewhere in the store.

The function of the EPOS terminal is to identify whatever is being bought by the shopper and pass this information to the central machine. This computer then returns the price and a brief description of the goods to the terminal which prints the customer's receipt. The customer can be provided with a fully itemised receipt listing what he or she has bought and its price. At the same time, the central machine maintains accounting information on the basis of information received from all of the EPOS terminals in the store. The central computer constantly monitors stock levels and as soon as the level of some particular item becomes low, an order for replacement supplies is issued.

Figure 5.3 is a photograph of an EPOS terminal being used in a supermarket to check out a customer's purchases.

Fig. 5.3   An EPOS terminal in use

An essential requirement for systems like this is
that it must be possible for the system to uniquely
identify each item which is sold. This means that
every terminal must include some way of discriminating
items and that each item must include some kind of
computer readable tag to identify it. Two tagging
techniques are presently in use - magnetic labelling
and bar coding.

Systems based on magnetic labelling must have each
item labelled with a tag which incorporates a strip of
magnetic material. A code which uniquely identifies
the particular item is recoded on this strip and this
can be read by a wand attachment connected to the EPOS
terminal.

Because such systems require each item to be
individually labelled, the cost of labelling is
relatively high. Not only are the labels themselves
expensive, but an assistant must be paid to carry out
the labelling process. This means that these systems
are most economic when used in conjunction with
relatively high-value goods. If a product is
expensive, the labelling cost is a tiny fraction of the
cost of the sale price of the product. Systems based
on magnetic labelling are not economic in shops like

supermarkets which deal mostly in lots of fairly low-cost purchases.

For supermarket systems, a tagging method based on bar codes is the most common labelling technique. A **bar code** is a series of varying width black and white stripes which is incorporated in the packaging of the goods. The bar code includes information about the manufacturer and the product . A European standard for bar codes has been universally agreed and more and more products include a bar code as part of the label. Figure 5.4 shows a bar code as it is printed on a product container.

Fig. 5.4   A laser scanning system

The bar code represents 13 digits which uniquely identify a particular product. The meaning of each group of digits is as follows:

(1)   Digits 1-2 indicate the country where the product is manufactured.

(2)   Digits 3-7 indicate the manufacturer.

(3)   Digits 8-12 indicate the particular product in that manufacturer's range.

(4)   Digit 13 is a so-called check digit used by the computer to check that the code has been read

correctly.

Bar codes may be read using a wand reader attached to the terminal or, alternatively, may be read by a special scanner which uses a laser to read and identify the bar code. A photograph of such a system, reading bar codes, is shown in Figure 5.4.

Although the scanner is much more expensive than a wand reader, it is also very much faster. The assistant need not pick up each product, orient it then slide the wand reader over the code. Rather, the item may simply be taken from the customer's basket with the bar code face down, and pushed over the scanner. The scanner can recognise a code at any angle and operates as fast as the assistant can slide items over it.

Irrespective of the labelling method used, the principles of operation of EPOS systems are the same. To operate such a system requires a central computer with all EPOS terminals connected directly to that machine. The central computer keeps in its memory a unique code for each item on sale, the price of the item and information about the sales of each item.

The tag on the product records the code for that particular purchase and the EPOS terminal reads this code and transmits it to the central computer. This system then looks up the price of that item in its memory, sends the price and product description to the terminal and adjusts the stock level for that particular item. When the EPOS terminal gets the price back from the central machine, it prints a receipt and adds that sum to a running total of items sold so far.

The advantages of this computerisation to the shopper are that, in theory at least, his or her waiting time at a supermarket checkout or sales point is reduced. Human error is eliminated so that accidental overcharging is impossible.

There are a number of advantages as far as the store is concerned. Stock control is improved, statistical information on sales can be readily obtained, fraud by checkout assistants is eliminated, labelling costs (in bar code based systems) are reduced, and price increases or reductions may be introduced without product relabelling.

Computer developments in retailing are not confined to large stores running complex and expensive computer systems. Small and medium size shops can also computerise their operations using microcomputer systems. It is already possible to buy a microcomputer controlled cash register which can 'remember' the names and prices of certain products. Rather than key in a price, the assistant inputs a code for the item being sold and the cash register system computes the price. The same cash register can be used by a number of assistants and it keeps track of sub-totals for each assistant. The system can also keep a record of sales on an ordinary cassette tape. This may be processed later by stock control programs.

A system like this is most useful in an environment which has lots of sales of relatively few distinct items. This means that assistants can remember the codes for each item. An example of such an environment is a local bar or pub and most examples of this type of system which are presently in use have been installed by breweries and publicans.

This is only one example of how computer technology may be used in small retail outlets but the potential for systems like this is almost limitless. It is certainly reasonable to predict that, by the year 2000, computerised shopping will be almost universal with all shops equipped with some kind of computer system.

5.3 THE CASHLESS SOCIETY

Developments in computerising financial and retail systems have led a number of commentators to suggest that cash will soon become an obsolete commodity and that all financial systems will be completely computerised.

In some respects, a move towards a cashless society is already underway. Many transactions nowadays use credit cards rather than cash or cheques. Many people use bank standing orders or direct debits to pay for regular outgoings such as mortgage repayments, subscriptions, etc. In this part of the book we consider if the total elimination of cash is a feasible proposition and if such a situation is indeed likely to come about.

5.3.1 Computerised shopping and EFT systems
As well as being used to read magnetic labels or bar codes on goods, the wand associated with EPOS terminals can also be used to read the magnetically encoded strip on bank cards or credit cards. This feature is already used by stores which operate their own credit card system. It can be used to check the validity of a card, check the customer's credit limits and to automatically debit the card holder's account as soon as a sale has been made.

In principle, such a system may be extended to national credit cards. When a sale is made, the store's computer could automatically telephone the credit company's computer and pass the credit card number to it. The validity of the card could be checked, the customer's account debited and a voucher automatically printed by the EPOS terminal for signature by the customer. This system would reduce the tedious waiting time required if credit is checked by telephone and may also eliminate certain types of credit fraud.

Such a system is simply an automated version of the

existing credit card system but other developments in computerised shopping may result in the integration of retail systems and electronic funds transfer systems (EFTS).

Rather than pay for shopping by cash or cheque, the customer may simply hand over his or her bank card. This will be read by a reader built into the EPOS terminal, the customer's bank will be automatically telephoned by the computer and a request made to transfer funds to the supermarket's account. If the bank's computer grants the request, the cost of the goods is automatically credited to the shop's account and the customer's account is debited.

Certainly such EFT systems are now technically possible. We shall probably see experimental trials of systems of this type in the near future. However, their introduction does present some problems.

One problem is that it is difficult for the customer to keep track of the amount of money which he or she has in his or her account. If the customer actually has to write a cheque, it is fairly natural to note the amount of that cheque and thereby be able to calculate what funds are available. If no actual writing is necessary, it is unrealistic to expect most people to note down all their transactions and to keep careful accounts.

This is not a serious problem until a situation arises where the funds in the account are inadequate for a particular purchase. Consider a situation where a customer in a supermarket selects a trolley-load of groceries, has them processed at the checkout and then attempts to pay for them via an EFTS. Say his or her account does not have enough in it to meet the cost of the groceries and the bank's computer refuses to authorise the funds transfer.

In such a situation it is probably unacceptable for the in-store computer simply to inform the checkout assistant of this who then must send the customer away empty-handed. Not only would this cause embarrassment and a breach of the customer's privacy - other customers would be able to deduce the state of his or her bank account - it would also involve supermarket staff replacing goods on the shelves. In the long run, it would almost certainly mean that the supermarket would have lost that customer for ever.

The only acceptable reaction in such a situation is to bill the customer for the goods and, perhaps, retain the EFTS card as security. However, this adds a new complication to the accounting system and negates some of the advantages of computerisation.

Another problem with such a system is that it will take a considerable time to convert all customers to the system. For all of that time, the EFTS must be run in parallel with existing cash based systems. The innate conservatism of the general public in money matters is such that this changeover period is likely to last decades unless there is some positive incentive to the customer to use EFTS. A possible incentive is, of course, a discount on the goods purchased and it is reasonable for the customer who pays by EFTS to expect this. After all, the use of such a system gives the shop immediate access to funds and should reduce accounting costs.

5.3.2 Replacing cash itself

Whilst it is possible to envisage EFTS being used for relatively large purchases in stores with powerful computer and communication systems, it seems unlikely that such systems will be used in smaller shops, pubs, and other environments where small amounts of cash change hands. In fact, it is really unthinkable that an EFTS system would be used to buy a newspaper, pay the fare for a short bus journey or buy a couple of drinks in the local pub.

For such purposes, we shall see the introduction of 'cash cards'. Cash cards will be the usual plastic card with a magnetic strip on which is recorded the value of the card. When a purchase is made, the customer's card will be put into a card reader terminal in the shop and the amount of the sale keyed in. This will be automatically deducted from the amount recorded on the card and added to the amount on the shop's card which will also be located in the terminal.

When the funds recorded on the card run out, the user will be able to 'recharge' it by using an automated teller terminal. He or she will be able to instruct the system to transfer funds from his or her bank account onto the card. Alternatively, if the card has had funds added to it, the teller system will be able to transfer these to the user's account.

One of the problems which must be overcome with such cards is the problem of making the value of the card visible to the user. This problem can probably be solved by building a simple microprocessor, a display and a rechargeable battery into each card. The micro would have a single function - displaying the amount left on the card - and users would be able to check that deductions and additions were accurate and would know when the card must be 'recharged' with funds.

The advantage of such a system is that it vastly reduces the amount of small change and notes which must be handled by shops and banks. It would speed up transactions by eliminating the need to give change, reduce the times pent by the shopkeeper in tedious cash accounting and reduce opportunities for fraud by shop staff.

However, the reluctance of the general public to change to new ways of working will probably make the introduction of such a system fairly slow. There are still old people in the UK who think in pounds, shillings and pence in spite of the fact that the conversion to decimal currency took place over ten years ago. It will be very difficult to convince people like that to convert to a system where cash is not actually visible and is simply represented as a number on a display.

To summarise this section on the cashless society, the elimination of cash and cheques is certainly technically feasible. There will be increasing pressure on the consumer by banks and shops to convert to such an economy. However, the conservatism of the general public is such that this will be a slow process and I think that it is safe to predict that, by the 21st century, cash will still play an important if lesser role in the economy.

5.4   THE SOCIAL IMPLICATIONS OF FINANCIAL AUTOMATION

As financial systems play such an important role in our society, any radical change in such systems is likely to have profound social implications. Almost the entire adult population makes use of financial systems and millions of people are employed by the financial institutions and in the retail sector of the economy. All of us will be affected, in one way or another, by changes to these systems.

One of the most significant and early changes which we shall see will be the universal use of bank accounts. At the time of writing, about 40% of the adult population of the UK do not have a personal bank account and clearly, any moves towards complete automation will require everyone to have such an account.

The pressure for universal banking will come jointly from the banks via hard-sell advertising and from employers who will refuse to pay wages and salaries in cash. The overheads in cash payments are so high that it will be economic for employers to financially reward employees who convert to direct payment into their bank account. This factor, along with improved automated banking services will mean that there is likely to be little resistance to this change. Similarly, pensions and state benefits will not be paid in cash but will be paid directly into a bank account.

The change to universal banking is likely to result in a blurring of the distinctions between banks and other financial institutions such as insurance companies, home loan societies, etc. There are two reasons for this:

(1)   The potential market is so great that, in order to expand, many financial institutions are likely

to offer banking services.

(2)   Once bank accounts are universal, banks can only
       expand by offering other financial services such
       as insurance and home loans.

This move towards generalised financial services is
already underway. In the UK, banks are competing
strongly with traditional building societies (home loan
societies) in the home loans market. Some building
societies are responding by offering banking services
such as cheque accounts and automated cash dispensers.
     As far as the public is concerned, these moves will
lead to increased competitiveness and, it is to be
hoped, better customer service. Banks and other
financial institutions have a conservative, rather
stuffy image which they are likely to attempt to change
using advertising and by offering real improvements in
service.
     The moves towards a cashless society will also
result in significant changes in the 'black economy'.
The 'black economy' is that part of the economy which,
at present, is completely cash based and undeclared to
the tax man. It is fairly common practice for trades
whose income is almost entirely cash, not to declare
part of that income. Some people take casual second
jobs, such as working evenings in a bar, without paying
tax on that income. As cash comes to play a lesser role
in the economy, such practices will become less
acceptable and more difficult to maintain. Because of
this, the existence of the 'black economy' may be a
significant constraint on the elimination of cash.
     It would be naive to imagine that the 'black
economy' will disappear as cash becomes used less and
less in our society. Rather, it is likely to change
from a cash based economy to a barter based economy.
Goods and services, rather than cash, will become the
medium of exchange. Small shops will trade groceries
for computer programming, window cleaning, etc. Casual
workers will be paid in goods. For example, a
decorator might paint the exterior of your house in
return for a new television set. Services will be
exchanged for services and goods for goods- babysitting
might be paid for by gardening, the butcher might pay
for his car repairs with cuts of meat.
     There are other very important implications of
financial automation. The nature of some kinds of
crime will change and this is discussed in the
following section. There will, almost certainly, be
technological unemployment in the financial and retail
sectors of the economy. Not only will there be fewer
jobs, but the jobs which are available will be highly
skilled and there will be few opportunities available
for those with minimal qualifications.

5.5   COMPUTERS AND CRIME

The advent of computerised financial systems has
already given opportunities for new and difficult-to-
detect forms of fraud. It is inevitable that, as such
systems become universal, more cases of computer fraud
will occur. However, this is not the only effect that
computerised financial systems will have on crime. In
this section, we shall look at computer fraud, the
vulnerability of computer systems to terrorist threats,
a completely new crime - software piracy, and the
effect on existing 'conventional' crime of moves
towards a cashless society.

5.5.1 Computer fraud

Any accounting system is vulnerable to fraud by
individuals who have an intimate knowledge of these
systems. Computer-based systems are no exception to
this. Although computer systems are less likely to be
defrauded by outsiders with less than complete
knowledge of the system, insiders who know the system
well can perpetuate frauds which are very difficult to
detect. The reason for this is that the majority of
auditors do not understand the details of computer
systems so can be fooled by the clever technical tricks
which an insider can use.

The scale of computer fraud is presently unknown -
not only are successful frauds undetected but frauds
which are detected are often 'hushed up' by the
organisations involved in order that confidence in
their business is not lost.

I shall illustrate how a computer may be used for
fraudulent purposes by presenting a couple of examples
of crimes which have actually happened. These examples
are typical of how computer frauds can be perpetrated
by introducing false data into a system and by altering
the programs which perform the system's computations.

Large organisations all trade with a variety of
other organisations who supply goods and services.
Invoices for these are normally processed by computer
and cheques printed in payment for these goods and
services. Generally, the invoice data is typed into the
computer system and the checking of whether goods have
been delivered or services received is carried out
against the invoices themselves rather than the
information in the system.

Frauds can occur if an insider can make use of this
information once it has been input to the computer but
before it has actually been processed. Phoney
companies can be set up and bills for non-existent
goods and services entered into the computer by the
defrauder. The computer then processes these false
entries and makes out cheques to these non-existent
companies who are, of course, simply a front for the
defrauder.

entries and makes out cheques to these non-existent companies who are, of course, simply a front for the defrauder.

In essence, this simplified case exemplifies the most common type of computer fraud. In practice, the perpetrators of the fraud are familiar with the details of the accounting system and can make their phoney entries very difficult to detect.

The second example shows how computer programs can be modified so that fraud can occur. Consider a program whose task is to compute the monthly salaries for all employees in a large organisation. Say a corrupt programmer changes that program so that after each salary is worked out, a small amount, say 5 pence, is deducted from that salary and added to the programmer's own salary. It is unlikely that anyone would notice the deduction of such a small sum, the books would balance, yet if there were 10 000 employees say, the programmer would earn an extra 500 pounds per month.

As computer and communication systems become more integrated, the potential for defrauding a system using its communication lines will increase. It may be possible to 'tap' a communication line, monitor the traffic on that line and deduce codes which allow payments to be made. Extra messages, including these codes, could then be entered on the line authorising payments to the defrauder.

What can be done to stop computer frauds? In general, it is probably impossible to make systems 100% secure and the insider with very detailed knowledge of a system will always be able to defraud that system, at least for a period of time. However, for all others, computer systems can include safeguards which make them much more secure than on-automated systems.

For example, any users of a particular piece of information may be required to know a secret password before being allowed access to that information, and every command, of any kind whatsoever, may be logged and analysed. Anomalous commands can be brought to the attention of the system auditors. It is possible to encrypt messages on communication lines so that they may not be readily decoded.

By building checks like these into computerised financial systems, most defrauders will be discouraged. Nevertheless, some defrauders will find ways to by-pass these checks. Because there will be so many more computerised financial systems in future, there will be more computer frauds than there are today.

5.5.2 Computers and terrorism

As day to day financial affairs of organisations become more and more dependent on computer systems, the vulnerability of these organisations to terrorist blackmail increases. Already, banks and other institutions cannot possibly afford to be without their

118

bombproof doors.

It is very likely that, in the near future, terrorists will take over some computer centre and threaten to destroy it, unless a large sum of money is paid to them. Sadly it is difficult to guard against this. In many cases it is practically impossible to fortify the computer centre and it is expensive and difficult to duplicate computer operations in some other site.

All that can be done to counter this threat is to maintain as strict security precautions as possible, to store copies of important data on some site apart from the computer centre and to have available contingency plans to buy time on another computer should the computer centre be destroyed.

5.5.3 Software piracy

Developing a reliable and efficient computer program is a time-consuming business and, as programmer time is not cheap, such programs are expensive to produce. The producer naturally wishes a return for his efforts and fixes a price for his program which depends on the number of copies of that system which he or she expects to sell.

A completely new crime which has resulted from the widespread use of computer systems is software piracy. Software piracy is the act of copying and using computer programs without paying the author or official seller of these programs for the copy. The practice is now widespread and perpetrated, often inadvertently, by many otherwise respectable and law-abiding organisations.

It is common practice for an organisation to buy a single copy of the program, make multiple copies itself, then distribute those within the organisation. This is quite illegal yet extremely difficult to detect. In fact, the person making the copies may not even know that he is acting illegally.

To deter software piracy, the designers of systems sometimes build in anti-copying features but no sooner are such features designed than a way is found to circumvent them. It is now even possible to buy software copying programs which guarantee to get round any anti-copying tricks used by the software producer.

The end result of this software piracy is, of course, that software producers are unwilling to invest time and effort to build reliable, easy-to-use software. This factor accounts for the relatively low quality of much microcomputer software which is presently available.

5.5.4 Crime and the cashless society

Computer-related crimes constitute an extremely small proportion of crimes which are committed today and,

excepting software piracy, this proportion seems
unlikely to increase. However, moves towards a
cashless society will have very significant effects on
existing crime patterns and I will try and predict some
of these effects here.

Most theft is geared towards obtaining cash for the
thief. This may be obtained directly by robbing a
bank, a shop, a pub, or by holding up a company's
payroll delivery. Alternatively, it may be obtained
indirectly by stealing goods and selling them for cash.
Cash therefore motivates a large proportion of existing
crime.

As more and more workers have bank accounts and
fewer and fewer companies make wage payments directly
in cash, the most immediate effect on crime will be
that there will be no scope for payroll robberies.
Furthermore, as stores make use of EFTS and credit
sales they will deal less in cash and the incentive for
robbing such stores will be diminished.

As computerised credit checking is established,
stolen credit cards will become valueless and the
criminal will be forced to confine his attentions to
those who continue to deal in cash. Sadly, this is
likely to be the most defenceless sector of society,
poor people and old people, and an unfortunate
consequence of computerising financial systems may be
increased attacks on these individuals.

The reduced size of the cash economy will mean that
there is likely to be more and more theft of goods –
housebreakings, shop robberies, etc. These goods can
then be exchanged for cash. A side effect of this is
that security businesses who lose trade because of the
reduction in cash deliveries will switch to property
protection as their main source of revenue.

In the longer term, as cash cards replace money for
small transactions, the amount of cash in the economy
will be further reduced. It may be that any cash
transactions will be looked upon with suspicion. As it
is possible to incorporate careful check on bank
accounts, the criminal would be likely to hesitate to
use his cash card to receive payment for stolen goods.
So, it is conceivable that the cashless society would
have a lower overall incidence of theft than exists at
present.

Whilst relatively low-value cash cards would be
unlikely to incorporate built-in security features, it
would be a trivial matter to incorporate such features
in high-value cards. Shop cards, which are credited
from each customer's card might be designed so that the
only allowed operation with that particular card is to
transfer the resources to the owner's bank account.
Therefore, there would be little point in stealing such
cards and hold-ups of small shops and pubs would become
a thing of the past.

Whilst the exact pattern of crime in a cashless society is difficult to predict, it is a reasonable forecast that life for the petty criminal at least, will become much more difficult. Organised crime however, cannot be suppressed so easily and will probably become more and more involved in schemes to defraud computer systems.

5.6   SUMMARY

Financial organisations were amongst the first users of computers and are now almost totally dependent on their computer systems. This chapter has looked at some of the uses made of information technology by banks, etc. and we have seen how, in future, cash could become an obsolete commodity. This has very significant social repercussions, particularly as far as crime is concerned. Accordingly, part of the chapter briefly examines the present and future relationship between computers and crime.

The use of computers by banks and stores offers important opportunities for these institutions to improve their customer services. Banks can provide automated teller terminals giving the customer access to some banking facilities outside normal banking hours. Stores can make use of point-of-sale systems to provide more information to the customer. These systems can also reduce customer waiting time by speeding up the process of paying for goods at a checkout or cash desk. They reduce the costs of running a store by providing better stock control and reducing pilferage.

A logical development of the use of computers by stores and banks is the provision of electronic funds transfer. Electronic funds transfer is a process where funds are automatically transferred from one bank account to another without any human intervention. A purchaser could buy goods in a store and pay for them simply by instructing the EFTS to complete the transaction. The store's computers and the bank's computer will make contact through a communications network and arrange for the cost of the goods to be transferred from the customer's account to the store's account.

Even cash itself may be replaced. Plastic cards might replace coins and notes. These cards would be 'charged' with some amount of money and as purchases are made, the buyer's card is debited and the seller's credited. This eliminates cash accounting, reduces the opportunities for theft, and eliminates the need for the seller to provide change. However, such innovations will not become universal for some time because of the innate conservatism of many people where money matters are concerned.

Moves towards a cashless society will have social

implications.   Everyone will have to have a bank
account.   Cash transactions made to avoid the seller
paying tax will disappear.   The nature of crime may
change.   Computer frauds will become more common where
the criminal attempts to swindle money by using a
computer.   Cash-related theft could disappear along
with cash itself. Petty criminals may find life more
difficult but organised crime will not disappear - it
will turn to computers instead.

Chapter 6
Microelectronics and medicine

Health care is now seen as a right in the developed
countries and this has resulted in increasing demands
being placed on medical services. In response to these
demands, sophisticated computer-controlled diagnostic
and monitoring instruments have been developed as aids
to the physician. Computers have come to play a crucial
role in the running of a modern hospital. The use of
computers is intended to increase the productivity of
medical staff allowing better care to be offered to a
greater number of patients without a disproportionate
increase in costs.

The large-scale administrative problems of running a
health-care system are comparable to those of any large
industry. Personnel must be paid, stocks purchased and
accounted for, ledgers maintained, etc. Furthermore,
information relating to patients, diseases, and
accidents must also be maintained and statistically
processed. Large mainframe computers have been used for
handling this type of work for a number of years and
the techniques used are comparable to those in
commercial data processing rather than exclusive to
medical administration. As this book is not concerned
with these data processing techniques, I shall not
discuss this aspect of medical computing. Rather, I
shall concentrate on the applications of relatively
small minicomputers and microprocessor systems in
patient care.

The topics which are covered are the use of
computers by family doctors and nurses, computer
systems which can diagnose illness automatically, and
the use of computers as controllers of other medical
equipment. The final section looks at computers and
bioengineering and discusses how computer controlled
devices can aid the handicapped and how microchips may
eventually be built into the human body itself.

Many developments in medicine have had a profound
social impact. For example, improved public hygiene
and immunisation against disease resulted in a
population boom; the invention of the oral
contraceptive was partly responsible for changes in
sexual behaviour which have taken place over the last
20 or so years.

Will, therefore, the widespread use of computers in medicine have comparable social effects? Computer systems will allow medical staff more time for patient care and relieve them of repetitive aspects of their work. However, they are unlikely to have a significant effect on birth or death rates nor will they change the habits of the general population. Computing will change medicine and allow better patient care. However, its social effects are unlikely to be as momentous as some previous developments in the history of medicine.

6.1   PATIENT INFORMATION SYSTEMS

Ideally information relating directly to the condition of patients should be immediately available to doctors and nurses. The most effective way to make this information instantly available is to store it on a computer which medical staff can use. The drop in price of computer systems means that it is now economic to install computers in hospital wards and doctors' surgeries. These systems provide information about patients for medical staff and can take over tedious form-filling duties from doctors and nurses. These patient care systems are the topic of this part of the book.

The basis of all such systems is the patient's medical record which contains an enormous amount of information. Starting from birth and ending with death, each and every consultation with a doctor is detailed in this record. It contains details of illnesses, drugs prescribed, laboratory test results, referrals to specialists, and so on, along with ancillary comments and remarks made by doctors and other medical staff.

Although some attempts have been made to completely computerise patient records, these have had only a limited degree of success. The reason for this is that the information in a medical record is unstructured and not recorded in a formal and consistent way. Records are usually made up of a mixture of handwritten and typewritten information and the task of converting all existing records to a form which can be read by a computer is enormous. Given money and time, the task is not actually insuperable but, as medical staff tend to be conservative in their working practices there is no real pressure to completely automate the record keeping system.

The systems which we shall look at here are not attempts to completely computerise record keeping but are means of supplementing the manual record system with up-to-date printed information about patients. They take over repetitive aspects of record maintenance and provide more timely information for doctors and nurses. The two types of system which will be discussed are administrative systems for family doctors which keep track of drugs prescribed to patients and nursing care systems for use in hospital wards.

6.1.1 Computers and the family doctor

Family doctors are usually the first contact which people have with the health care system and they are normally organised into fairly small local practices. The size of these practices is such that they cannot afford large capital investments in equipment so, until the advent of the microcomputer, there was no possibility of automating any of the work of the local general practitioner.

Even now, with microcomputers readily available, there are only a few family doctors making use of computers. There reasons for this are:

(1)   Doctors share the general public's ignorance of computer systems and see them as difficult to use and understand.

(2)   Many if not most doctors in general practice were trained before computers played any part in medi-cine and do not realise that the machines can reduce their workload.

(3)   Those doctors and nurses who do understand that computers can help them have no time to write computer programs. As a result, there are hardly any off-the-shelf computer programs available to help other medical staff.

This situation is almost certain to change over the next few years as curricula in medical schools include courses in medical computing and as more programs are developed to help the family doctor.

There is a great deal that computers can do to lighten the administrative load on general practitioners and their staff. For instance, appointments systems can be computerised so that receptionists can immediately tell patients when an appointment with a particular doctor is available. Word processors can be used to handle correspondence, and a computer system can be developed to handle routine drug prescriptions.

Many patients on a family doctor's list take one or more drugs on a continuing basis and prescriptions for new supplies of these drugs must be issued regularly. The majority of these patients are elderly and typically suffer from a number of complaints. They may take several drugs to control blood pressure, rheumatism, arthritis, diabetes, etc. When a patient takes a number of drugs an important factor which the physician must take into account is the interactions of these drugs with each other. Some drugs suppress the effects of others and some magnify the effects so that it is important that the patient is not prescribed a combination of drugs which will have adverse side effects. Furthermore, when the patient is issued prescriptions at regular intervals, the physicians should be able to check that the patient is taking the correct dose of each drug.

The cost of drugs is very high and is a factor which most doctors take into account irrespective of whether these drugs are being paid for by the patient, medical insurance, or a national health service. Many identical versions of the same drug are available under different names at widely differing costs so if a particular drug is needed, the physician should try to prescribe the cheapest example of it.

As there are several hundred drugs in common use it is a difficult task to keep track of drug costs and drug interactions. Most doctors know dangerous interactions and names of common drugs but cannot always remember relative costs or obscure drug side effects. It is unrealistic to expect doctors to keep such a mass of information in their heads but, by using a computer, interactions and costs can be catalogued and instantly retrieved.

When a patient starts a course of medication, the drugs prescribed can be entered along with patient details into the computer system. The system then checks that there are no adverse drug interactions. If there are, it can advise the doctor of alternatives. The machine also keeps a note of drug costs. The doctor need not remember the cheapest version of a particular drug but can prescribe any version whatsoever. The computer checks to see if an identical but cheaper version of the drug is available under a different name. If so, it replaces the prescribed name with the cheaper alternative.

When a patient requests a new supply of his or her drugs, the prescription is automatically printed by the computer for signature by the doctor. The receptionist need only type the patients name and address into the system and need not look up records to find which drugs the patient needs. To help the doctor, a set of warnings may be printed along with the prescription if the patient requests a drug too often, too rarely or at irregular intervals.

Such a computer system also has other advantages. It provides printed information about the drugs which the patient takes and this is filed with the patient's medical record. The computer can also maintain a record of consultations with the doctor so that both the doctor and the patient can be reminded when a review of medication is due. Finally, the computer can process the drug and patient information to gather statistics about how many patients take particular drugs, etc.

Systems such as this one have an important part to play in the local doctor's surgery. They increase efficiency and reduce costs. Moreover, they improve the quality of patient care by bringing important information to the attention of the doctor in a timely way.

6.1.2 Nursing care systems

Each patient in a hospital ward has a nursing care schedule. This schedule sets out which drugs are to be administered, which tests are due or have been carried out, which specimens are to be collected and any special requirements which the patient may have.

These schedules can be implemented in two ways. Either each patient has an individual schedule describing the complete care that they require or lists are maintained of which patients require each aspect of nursing care. In such cases, individual care schedules can be found out by checking all lists.

In British hospitals, at least, the majority of nursing care schedules are held as these task lists because it simplifies the organisational problems of the nurse in charge of the ward. A list of all patients who are due to have blood pressure tested, say, is prepared and a nurse goes round these patients carrying out these tests one after another. Changes to the care needed by a particular patient are made by adding or deleting that patient's name from the appropriate task list.

Although this system is convenient from the organisational point of view, it is not convenient from the point of view of an individual patient. All information about him or her is not gathered together on the same piece of paper. Hence, it is difficult for a doctor or nurse to get an overall picture of the nursing care devoted to a patient and to assess if that care needs to be modified. Nurses prefer individual schedules as they allow all tasks associated with a particular patient to be carried out at the same time and they allow the nurse to establish a good working relationship with that patient.

It is tedious and time consuming to prepare individual nursing care schedules by hand. However, it is a straightforward matter to maintain details of nursing care on a computer and to print either task lists or individual care schedules.

To implement such a system, each ward in a hospital must be equipped with a small computer system. Each ward computer must also be able to communicate with others so that patient information can be passed from one machine to another. When a patient is admitted to a particular ward, personal details are entered into the computer along with the required nursing care information. The system can then print a personalised care schedule for that patient.

Should the patient's requirements change, the changes are input to the nursing care systems and a revised schedule issued immediately. When a patient is discharged from the hospital, the nursing care computer scans that patient's record and summarises the nursing care provided. This summary is then included in the patient's complete medical record.

If necessary, the system can also process each patient's nursing care record and generate task lists. However, experience with such a system in a Scottish hospital has shown that nurses prefer personal care schedules rather than task lists and little use is made of this facility.

As well as allowing nurses to work from these individual care plans, nursing care systems have a number of other advantages:

(1)   Relief nursing staff or staff who have been off-duty can be brought up-to-date on the care required by particular patients. This involves recalling care plans from the computer. Given the time when a nurse went off duty say, the system provides details of all patient care plans which have changed since then.

(2)   The information provided by the system is useful for nurse training as each patient's care schedule is kept with the patient so that trainees can be shown what is required and how to carry out particular tasks.

(3)   Given the care schedules for every patient, the work required in any particular ward can be computed. Nurses' duty rotas can therefore be scheduled so that there are always enough nurses to carry out the tasks which have to be done at any particular time.

Such nursing care systems have been introduced in a number of hospitals and have been well received by nurses who soon become used to using a computer terminal installed in the ward. These systems and family doctor systems are good examples of how automation can lighten the administrative load placed on medical staff and allow them to concentrate on improved patient care.

6.2   COMPUTER-AIDED DIAGNOSIS

When a patient feels ill and visits his or her family doctor for advice, the doctor can take a number of different actions:

(1)   He can reassure the patient that his or her com-
        plaint is not serious and does not require any
        medication.

(2)   He can prescribe drugs or treatment for the pa-
        tient in order to counteract a particular condi-
        tion.

(3)   He can refer the patient to another doctor, usu-
        ally in a hospital or clinic, who can give the
        patient specialist advice and treatment. This
        course of action is usually taken when the doctor
        is not completely sure of what is wrong with the
        patient.

It is probable that most of the cases which a general
practitioner must deal with are fairly minor illnesses.
They do not need referral to a specialist but either
clear up naturally or can be readily treated by the
family doctor. However, there is a significant minority
of patients who are suffering from more serious
complaints. These patients need further advice and
treatment. Sometimes it is not immediately clear
whether a patient is suffering from a minor illness or
whether he or she ought to be referred for further
treatment. In such cases, the doctor must spend quite
a lot of time questioning the patient to find out the
background to his or her illness and to establish any
ancillary symptoms which might exist. On the basis of
this information, the doctor must them make a decision
on whether or not specialist advice is required.

The problem is, of course, that family doctors must
be generalists and cannot possibly know the symptoms of
every possible condition. They must use their limited
knowledge as best they can and not take chances with
the patient's health. However, the opportunity now
exists to encapsulate specialist knowledge in a
computer program which can be used by the doctor to
help him make decisions on whether or not the patient
needs further advice and treatment.

This computer-aided diagnosis system is based on a
standard microcomputer equipped with a special
simplified keyboard. This keyboard has only numeric
keys plus three keys labelled 'yes', 'no' and 'don't

know'. The computer asks the patient a number of questions which he or she answers by pressing the appropriate key. These questions are phrased in a simple, non-technical way which can be understood by most patients and which the patient can answer with a 'yes' or a 'no' or with a number. For instance, typical questions from a system intended to diagnose gastro-intestinal conditions are:

(1)   Do you feel very full or 'bloated' after every meal?

(2)   Do you drink more than 6 measures of spirit such as whisky, gin or vodka in a day?

(3)   How many months have you had these symptoms?

Once the computerised interviewing session is complete, the computer prints a summary of the patient's answers for the doctor along with its own diagnosis of what is wrong with the patient. This diagnosis is not an absolute diagnosis such as 'Patient X has a peptic ulcer' but is a list of possible conditions along with a probability that the patient is suffering from each particular condition. The doctor then uses this information to help him make his own diagnosis of what is wrong with the patient.

Experience with using a system of this type in parallel with the normal specialist referral mechanism has shown that it is actually 'better' in some areas than the average family doctor in deciding whether or not a patient should get further treatment. Although the idea of a computer being 'better' than a doctor is a bit unreal, what it means is that the system didn't miss any patients who really needed to see a specialist. Moreover, it didn't make so many unnecessary referrals as the family doctor. This means a real saving in time, money, and the patient's anxiety and inconvenience.

As well as reducing unnecessary referrals, automated patient interviewing also has several other advantages:

(1)   It saves the doctor time as it avoids him having to go through a lengthy interviewing process himself. It also makes sure that no important questions are inadvertently missed out by the physician.

(2)   Patients seem to like to use the system and some even prefer it to a personal interview with the doctor. The reason for this is that the computer appears to be both friendly and approachable and not in any way superior to the patient. In a personal interview, many patients particularly if

130

they are from deprived backgrounds, are in awe of
the doctor's education and abilities. They feel
that they are wasting his time if they hesitate
over an answer or are unsure what a question actually means. With the computer however, they
have no such qualms. They always feel that they
are in control of the interviewing session.

(3)   Patients seem to be more honest with the computer
than they are with a doctor where questions which
reflect on their 'image' are concerned. For example, when patients with alcohol related problems
were interviewed by computer they consistently
admitted to drinking more to the computer than
they did in a personal interview. The reason for
this is the same as that above - they feel in
control of the interviewing session and they
don't think that they have some 'image' to
preserve.

As well as being used directly by patients, computer-
aided diagnosis systems are also used by medical staff.
These systems are basically the same as patient
interviewing systems but, obviously, the questions can
be terse and phrased in technical terms understood by
the doctor.
    Experience with using these systems with junior
doctors in an emergency unit showed that again the
computer is better than the doctor in avoiding
unnecessary treatment. However, as the doctor gains
experience with the system, this discrepancy is reduced
and sometimes eliminated. The computer-aided diagnosis
system acts as a training aid for the doctor so that he
or she learns more about symptoms and their causes as
he or she makes use of the computer.
    The basis of all of these computer-aided diagnosis
systems is a record of symptoms and the associated
probability that the symptom is due to a particular
condition. The system questions the patient or doctor
to find out if a symptom is present. If so, it
'remembers' this as it continues with the questioning.
At the end of the session, the computer looks at all
the probabilities and multiplies them together to give
the final probability that the patient suffers from a
particular condition. A list of possible illnesses and
the probability of each is printed at the end of the
interviewing session.
    Because the approach taken to the problem of
computer-aided diagnosis is fairly simple, these
diagnosis systems can run on a cheap microcomputer
which can be installed anywhere that there is a power
supply. They don't need highly trained staff to
operate them so they can be used by medical auxiliaries
as well as doctors. At the time of writing, computer-

aided diagnosis systems like those described here are standard equipment on US submarines which do not normally carry a doctor on board. If a potentially critical situation arises, para-medical staff use the system to assess the seriousness of the patient's condition. If he requires more expert treatment, the submarine can make for port or can surface and allow the patient to be picked up by helicopter.

There have been a number of computer-aided diagnosis systems built which do not rely entirely on statistical probability. Rather, these systems try to emulate a doctor's diagnostic techniques where built in knowledge of conditions is used. When a doctor decided what is wrong with a patient, he or she doesn't compute probabilities but uses knowledge of illnesses and related symptoms to decide what is wrong with the patient.

Computer systems which use this approach are called knowledge-based systems or sometimes, expert systems. They can cope with a greater range of illnesses and symptoms than simple probability-based computer-aided diagnosis programs. These knowledge-based programs are large and complex and make use of a large data base of information concerning the particular medical speciality under study.

The principles which underlie knowledge-based systems are covered in Chapter 7 and, it is likely that this type of system will soon become fairly widely used. Experience of these knowledge-based systems has shown that not only are they much better than the average GP or junior doctor, they are actually better than most specialists in accurately diagnosing illness.

So far, the computer-aided diagnostic techniques which have been discussed are based on the patient answering questions about his or her condition. On the basis of the patient's replies, the computer comes up with its diagnosis. We shall now look at a complementary diagnostic technique where the computer processes automatically collected information about the patient such as information on heart functioning or breathing rates.

An electrocardiogram (ECG) is a graphical record of the contractions of the muscles in the heart. It is taken by attaching electrodes to the patient's body and detecting changes in electrical activity in the heart itself. The ECG of a healthy heart is very distinctive whereas heart defects show up as irregularities of one kind or another in the pattern of this ECG. The particular nature of these irregularities depends on what is wrong with the heart so the cardiologist can use the ECG to help diagnose specific heart conditions.

As different heart conditions have distinctive patterns of irregularity, the relationship between irregularities and heart defects can be stored in a computer. When an ECG is taken, it can then be analysed by the computer and compared with these stored ECGs. When a match is found, the computer can then identify the heart defect.

This automatic analysis of ECGs has a number of advantages compared to the manual system where the doctor looks at a graph and relates its shape to his previous experience. These are:

(1)   The computer can carry out the analysis more quickly, more reliably, and more cheaply than a human doctor.

(2)   The cost of periodically screening patients for heart disease is reduced. Rather than requiring the services of a doctor who analyses the ECG, all that is required is a nursing technician to connect the patient to the computer. After a relatively short time, a diagnosis can be produced by the machine. If the system detects an irregularity in the ECG, it can advise the patient to seek further advice. Such systems will make routine ECG checking economic and will allow potentially serious heart disease to be detected at an early stage.

(3)   For patients who may be ill and live far from a large hospital, a portable ECG machine can be used by their family doctor. The ECG can be taken and transmitted by telephone to a computer in remote department of cardiology, the ECG can be analysed and the results returned immediately to the family doctor. The computer may also suggest how to treat the patient and whether he or she should be brought to hospital. This approach would save tiring and expensive journeys to and from hospital for those patients who can be adequately treated at home.

Computer-aided diagnosis systems of one kind or another have great potential. They offer opportunities for improving diagnoses, reducing costs and allowing preventative medicine to be practiced where potentially serious illnesses are detected and cured in their early stages.

At the same time, however, they do pose some problems for medical staff. Firstly, there is no doubt that some doctors will see them as a threat taking away their traditional skills. They will probably resist them for that reason. Secondly, when the computer makes a diagnosis which is wrong, who should take responsibility - a computer cannot be sued for its mistakes!

There is no doubt at all that computerised systems

have taken over a number of traditional skills. Clerical work, typesetting, machine control are all examples of skills which are better done by computer and, some time in future, the computer may take over the diagnosis of illness from doctors. Already machines make fewer misdiagnoses than junior doctors and with some refinement they will outperform middle-level consultants. Only the most senior medical staff are not really threatened as they can deal with obscure and unusual complaints. The computer would not consider these because it is probably not worth including details of these very rare illnesses in the computerised system.

Not only will computer-aided diagnosis systems make fewer mistakes than doctors, the time may come when patients prefer to consult with such a system rather than with a doctor. This is particularly likely in situations where, for some reason, the patient is ashamed of his or her condition. Going further, should these computerised diagnosis systems be developed so that they offer advice on treatment as well as diagnoses, we may even see the emergence of do-it-yourself medicine where the patient need have no contact at all with the doctor. Rather, he or she will use an automated medical centre to obtain diagnosis and treatment of his or her complaint.

Naturally, developments like these affect both the self-image and the public image of doctors. Doctors are rightly proud and jealous of their skills and they have established a system which forbids anyone to practice medicine without a long, supervised period of training. It certainly is a blow to their self-esteem if a computer costing a few thousand pounds or dollars can do a better job than they can and is actually preferred by the patients! Furthermore, the public image of doctors as gurus who rarely make mistakes is likely to be shattered if the public see doctors being replaced by a computer similar to the one they have at home to play games.

Because computing is not an important part of medical training, because of the threat to the doctor's image, and because if the reluctance of doctors to change traditional ways of working, I think that the introduction of computer-aided diagnostic system will be resisted by some medical staff. Indeed, this resistance is already apparent in some hospitals where such systems have been introduced. Unless clearly instructed to make use of these computer, most doctors pay no attention to them. They impose a formal approach to diagnosis which differs from the informal, intuitive approach which is more familiar.

This resistance to computer system is short sighted. Although computer systems may take over much of the diagnosis of disease there are many other aspects of

medicine where doctors can practice their skills.
Unlike print workers, say, whose job has been largely
taken over by computerised typesetting, it is extremely
unlikely that doctors will be completely replaced by
computers. Rather, they may have to change the
emphasis of their job. They will have time to
concentrate on preventitive rather than curative
medicine and to develop treatment for rare diseases.
This can only be of benefit to the whole community.

There is, however, a problem associated with
computerised diagnosis which must be resolved before
these systems can be allowed to take over from doctors.
That is the problem of allocating responsibility when
such a system makes a mistake.

At the moment, computers are not used on their own
to make diagnoses but are used to help doctors to make
decisions. However, one of the advantages of these
systems is that they can be used in remote locations
far away from doctors such as ships at sea, oil rigs,
or in remote parts of the country. Inevitably, in such
situations the system user has to trust in its
diagnosis.

Furthermore, as these systems become commonplace
they will become more and more accepted and trusted by
medical staff in the same way as medical equipment such
as X-ray machines is regarded as reliable and correct.
Therefore, in future, for many patients it is probable
that the ultimate diagnosis will be made by machine
rather than by a human doctor.

Almost certainly, computer systems will make fewer
mistakes than doctors when they formulate diagnoses as
the systems will be designed always to err on the side
of caution. Mistakes may lead to unnecessary treatment
but will not mean that treatment is withheld.
Inevitably, however, there will be some mistakes made -
who is to be held responsible for them?

The easy answer to this question is to say that
there is some doctor in charge of the department which
runs the diagnostic computer and that he or she is
ultimately responsible for any mistakes made by the
machine. This is all very well if that doctor has been
the expert who 'trained' the machine but if he didn't
actually have anything to do with it, shouldn't the
original 'experts' be the ones to blame?

Probably the best approach is for health authorities
to accept that computers will make occasional mistakes
and they should set up some mechanism for compensating
those who are affected. After all, if some other piece
of medical machinery inadverently fails and a patient
suffers, a doctor is not necessarily held responsible
for this. Rightly or wrongly, however, people do see
computers as being different from other kinds of
machine and we must take this into account otherwise
compensation problems might arise.

6.3 REAL-TIME MEDICAL SYSTEMS

A computer system which can gather information from a set of sensors, process that information then initiate a series of actions which depend on the sensor input is called a **real-time computer system**. Real-time systems are used in a wide variety of applications from controlling domestic washing machines to piloting jet aircraft.

In medicine, there is enormous scope for using such systems but the only really widespread medical application of real-time systems which has been developed is in radiology. Computerised systems can form images from X-rays, gamma rays or very high frequency sound waves and allow the doctor to 'see' the interior of the body so that diagnoses can be made and treatment monitored.

The principal constraint on the development of medical real-time systems until recently has been the cost of computers. The systems require a computer for each patient being treated so many machines are required for a comprehensive system. As well as the cost of these machines, the physical size of minicomputers restricted the number of instruments in which they could be incorporated.

Now, with small and cheap microprocessor-based systems, real-time systems in medicine look set to become an essential part of hospital equipment. Computerised systems will be used to monitor patients who are seriously ill or who are undergoing some temporary crisis such as an operation or childbirth. Not only will these systems watch over patients, they will also be able to alert doctors and to initiate other machines to take corrective action when potentially dangerous situations are detected. This type of system and computerised imaging systems are the topics which are covered in this section.

6.3.1 Monitoring and control systems
When a patient is critically ill, undergoing surgery or giving birth, it is important to watch over that patient so that indications of danger can be picked up as early as possible. On such indications, corrective treatment can be initiated. For example, if a patient who suffers from a heart condition has a sudden change in blood pressure, this may indicate that some kind of heart attack is imminent and that treatment to correct this should be started right away.

The task of monitoring patients is a labour intensive and wearisome job. The nurse responsible can usually do nothing else but wait for something to happen and, in many cases, nothing ever happens and the nurse's time is completely wasted. As danger signs are quite obvious and well-defined in many cases, this is an obvious area for computerisation where patient monitoring is taken over by an automated system.

Computer monitoring systems are systems which watch over patients by collecting sensor data and checking it for indications of dangerous conditions. If danger is detected, the system can alert medical staff to take action. Monitoring and control systems are a development of simple monitoring systems where the computer itself initiates the actions needed to treat the patient's condition.

We shall look at two different systems which typify the current state of patient monitoring systems. As an example of a monitoring system, I shall describe a system which watches over patients who have recently had a heart attack. Monitoring and control systems are exemplified by a computerised pancreas used for treating diabetic patients undergoing surgery or some other crisis.

We have already seen how a computer-aided diagnosis system can analyse a patient's ECG, detect abnormalities and suggest diagnoses of heart defects. A cardiological monitoring system is based in similar principles. Each patient has permanently attached sensors which detect his or her heart's activity. The output from these sensors is fed to a microprocessor system for individual monitoring and it is passed from there for display on a central console. This central console is watched over permanently by a nurse. If the microprocessor monitoring the ECGs detects any abnormal changes in the patient's heart, it can send a message to the central computer which sets off an alarm at the nurse's console. If the abnormality is serious, it might also alert doctor's rooms elsewhere in the building. Medical help can thus be immediately summoned for the patient.

The advantages of a system like this compared to a system where a nurse sits with each patient are quite clear. With the help of computers, a single nurse can watch over a number of patients and need not even spend all her time watching the ECG display. She can get on with other jobs and rely on the alarm system to tell her if a patient is in need of attention.

Cardiological monitoring equipment cannot, by itself, initiate other equipment to treat a patient. However, there are some situations where treatment is well-defined and requires only simple equipment such as an automatic drug injection system. An example of such a situation is in the treatment of diabetics who may need injections of either insulin or glucose.

Diabetes is a condition which effects the pancreas and which hinders or retards the body's ability to produce insulin. Insulin is a chemical which is necessary to break down sugars in the blood so that energy is generated for the muscles of the body.

Diabetics, therefore, must inject artificial insulin daily so that their blood sugar can be utilised. Excessively high or low blood sugar levels are very dangerous so the amount of insulin taken by a diabetic must be carefully controlled.

This control is normally carried out by coordinating insulin injections with eating. However, in situations where eating is not advised or impossible such as prior to or during surgery, an alternative control mechanism must be used. An artificial pancreas is a monitoring and control system which is designed for this purpose.

The artificial pancreas works by taking very small samples of the patient's blood at regular intervals and analysing these to estimate the blood sugar level. If this level is within the normal, safe range the system takes no action but if it is either too high or too low the machine automatically corrects the sugar level in the blood. It does this by injecting either insulin to break down sugar if the level is high or glucose to provide sugar if the level is low.

The monitoring system has two small injection pumps attached to it with associated reservoirs of insulin and glucose. When the system detects a high sugar level, it sends a signal to the insulin pump to inject a small amount of insulin. Conversely, if the level is low, the glucose pump is started to inject sugar and bring the level back to within the safe range.

These are typical systems which are now in use but they really represent only the tip of the iceberg as far as potential uses of medical real-time systems are concerned. With microprocessors, many different systems are now possible and will relieve nursing staff of wearisome duties and give early warning of critical situation. We may even see such systems built into the body itself. This possibility is explored in a later section of this chapter.

6.3.2 Computerised imaging systems

The discovery of X-rays at the end of the 19th century marked an extremely important step forward for medical science. For the first time, doctors were not restricted to deducing internal problems from the outside but could actually see the state of the inside of the body.

X-rays are not true interior pictures but are shadowgraphs. The X-rays from the X-ray source pass through a part of the body and are absorbed by the tissues in the body. Different types of tissue absorb different amounts of X-rays. Bone, for example, is more absorbent of X-rays than muscle tissue and abnormalities such as tumours often also have different X-ray absorption characteristics from normal surrounding tissue. Hence X-rays show up breaks in bones or defects in lungs or indeed anything where the

differential absorbtion of X-rays is related to illness
or abnormality.

Conventional flat plate X-rays are now an essential
diagnostic tool but they suffer from three important
disadvantages:

(1)   They can only be used to take side-on pictures of
       parts of the body where the X-ray source is
       placed at one side and the camera at the other.
       There is no way they can be used to look at long-
       itudinal cross-sections or slices of a patient's
       body.

(2)   Some internal organs are composed entirely of
       soft tissue and abnormalities in these organs may
       not show up clearly in X-rays. This means that
       X-rays are not useful in diagnosing problems with
       these particular organs.

(3)   X-rays are high-power radiation and can actually
       cause tissue damage particularly in unborn ba-
       bies. Therefore, they cannot be safely used to
       follow the progress of a pregnancy.

To counter these limitations of flat plate X-rays a
number of different computerised imaging systems have
been developed. Some of these use gamma rays from
radioactive tracer chemicals and others make use of
ultra-high frequency sound waves.

Although these imaging systems vary considerably in
detail and implementation, they all operate on the same
fundamental principle. Radiation from some source is
picked up on an array of detectors. The intensity of
this radiation is directly related to internal body
structure. A computer system picks up the detector
output and uses it to create an image of the particular
part of the body which is being examined.

The generation of an image is based on the same
principle as television. A complete image is created by
considering it to be made up of many small distinct
elements which are given the name pixels, standing for
'picture element'. These elements are arranged in a
rectangular or square array where there are about 300
horizontal lines with 300 elements in each line. This
means that a complete image is made up of 90 000
distinct picture elements.

Each and every pixel has a value associated with it
which represents a shade of grey on the final image.
This pixel value is worked out by the computer by
analysing the intensity of the radiation which has
passed through the area of the body corresponding to
the pixel on the computer-generated image. A photograph
of such an image produced by an X-ray scanning machine
is shown in Figure 6.1.

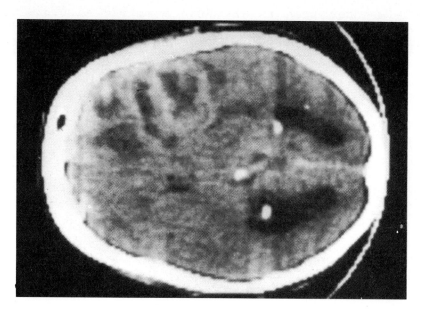

Fig. 6.1   A computer generated image

Once the computer has worked out the intensity values for every pixel in the image, the image itself can then be displayed on a screen like a TV screen. The image is a monochrome image with abnormalities showing up as lighter or darker areas in healthy tissue.

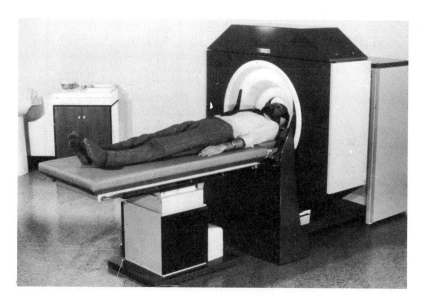

Fig. 6.2   An X-ray scanner

As an illustration how these imaging systems work, I shall describe in very general terms the workings of an X-ray scanner such as that shown in Figure 6.2. This type of machine is now widely used in hospitals in order to obtain special types of X-ray.

The function of an X-ray scanner is to obtain X-rays of cross-sectional areas of the body or head. The system operates with the patient lying still on a bed and with the X-ray source and associated X-ray detectors moving right round the patient. Because the machine rotates through 360 degrees, X-rays pass through a complete slice of the patient's body. Figure 6.3 is a diagram of this process where the patient's head is being X-rayed.

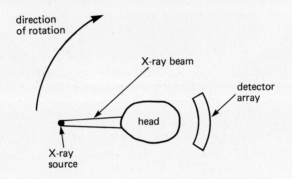

Fig. 6.3   X-ray scanning

The X-ray source gives out a fan shaped beam of X-rays and this source rotates around the patient in time with a detector array. The detector output is fed continuously to the controlling computer. As this rotation takes place, the computer picks up X-ray intensities as the beam passes through each part of the head. Because the X-ray beam is fan shaped, X-rays pass through each part of the head from many different positions and, depending on the angle, there will be a different pixel intensity value computed for each position. The job of the computer is to take all of these intensity values and put them together to form a final composite intensity and display this for the doctor or technician.

The various computerised imaging systems have made a tremendous difference to diagnostic medicine. Before these systems were invented, doctors had to perform exploratory surgery to diagnose many internal disorders or, indeed, were unable to diagnose them at all until they became acute. They represent an important advance in patient care.

6.4   THE AUTOMATION OF MAN

An idea beloved of science fiction writers is that of the cyborg or bionic man - a symbiosis of man and machine which combines the best features of the human and the machine. Although the extreme examples put about by science fiction writers such as men with superhuman strength or spaceships controlled by preserved organic brains are somewhat far-fetched, medical technology has now reached the stage where it is technically possible to build microprocessors into the human body itself.

The heart is a complex organ made up of a number of parts which must operate together to pump a regular flow of blood around the body. Certain heart conditions affect the synchronism of the various parts of the heart. These conditions can often be corrected by installing a heart pacemaker which produces a timing signal making sure that all parts operate at the right time.

The first pacemakers were relatively simple machines without any inbuilt decision making capability. They could only really deal with a single type of heart abnormality. Recently, however, new pre-programmed pacemakers incorporating a microprocessor have been developed which can identify changing states in the heart and can react accordingly. Effectively a real-time control system as discussed earlier in this chapter can be implanted within the body to control the timing of heartbeats.

Another application of microprocessors to supplement and replace parts of the body is helping sufferers from cerebral palsy to communicate. Cerebral palsy is a very disabling condition which affects that part of the brain which governs muscular control. Sufferers from cerebral palsy have limited muscular control and often cannot speak intelligibly. For this reason, they are sometimes thought to be mentally retarded although, in fact, the rest of their brain is quite normal and those with this condition have the same range of intellectual abilities as exists in the rest of the population.

Cerebral palsy sufferers often have virtually no control over their muscles - they may only be able to control the toes of one foot, head movements, or sometimes even just eye movements. Fortunately however, these very elementary movements can sometimes be used to operate a microprocessor-based speech synthesis system which can talk for its user. Codes representing each word are stored by the system so that inputting a particular code causes that word to be spoken. The codes can either be input through a keyboard worked by the toes, the nose or through a blowpipe. Alternatively, they can be picked up by a detector system which identifies particular muscle movements and relates these to word codes.

There are countless examples of potential systems where microprocessor-based devices operate in conjunction with the human body. The notion of an artificial pancreas controlling the blood sugar of diabetics has already been discussed. There seems to be no reason why such a system cannot ultimately be miniaturised and permanently worn by diabetics. Similarly, the same techniques might be applicable to other glands in the body.

More radically, computerised systems might be used to pick up signals from the brain to the muscles and convert these neuro-muscular signals into actions. This would be of enormous benefit to wearers of artificial limbs as the limb could become an active working limb rather than a passive object attached to the body.

Our normal limb functioning depends on signals sent from the brain via the nervous system. These signals contain encoded muscular instructions such as 'grasp' or 'bend'. There is evidence to suggest that even when someone loses a limb, he or she does not lose the capacity to transmit these signals. In principle, it should be possible to build 'intelligent' artificial limbs which use implanted sensors to detect these neuro-muscular signals and small electric motors to move the limb in response to these signals. This means that, ultimately, it should be possible to provide those disabled by the loss of a limb with artificial replacements which are almost as flexible as natural limbs.

Even more radically, it may be possible to pick up thoughts directly from the brain and use these to control other machinery. Micro-sensors would be imbedded in the skull and brain wave patterns interpreted by a microprocessor built into a helmet or other headgear. This could be very useful for some very complex tasks such as flying a plane at supersonic speeds as it would allow actions to be initiated without manual intervention. However, the time between thinking about an action and actually carrying it out is useful as it gives the brain a brief interval to decide if the action is sensible or not. We often decide to do something then change our minds before actually carrying it out. Thought controlled systems should therefore have some kind of built in delay to allow a thought to be 'cancelled' before irrevocable action is taken.

Similar techniques could be used to take the output from computerised sensors and directly stimulate parts of the brain. For example, blind people could be fitted with vision sensors which mimic the functions of the eyes and which feed information directly to the optic nerve. Those afflicted by deafness could use audio sensors in place of ears with the sensor output fed directly to the part of the brain which interprets aural signals.

The automation of man is at a very early stage and it will be many years before developments such as those outlined above come into common use. Bionic men are perhaps unlikely but microprocessor systems will have an important role to play in controlling potentially dangerous conditions and in helping the disabled play a full role in society.

6.5   SUMMARY

Until fairly recently, the use of computers in medicine was almost exclusively restricted to administration. Now, the advent of the microprocessor means that computer systems are cheap enough to be included in hospital wards and doctors' surgeries. They can be dedicated to implementing patient care systems.

The first part of this chapter looks at two different kinds of patient care system. The first of these is a system for use by a family doctor. This handles the issuing of repeat prescriptions to patients who take continuous medication. Not only does the system relieve medical staff of the tedious task of writing these prescriptions, it can also provide timely information to the doctor about when drugs are issued to patients.

The second patient care system considered here is a nursing care system. This system is installed in a hospital ward and provides details of the nursing care required by each patient. As well as allowing individual patient care schedules to be produced, nursing care systems also simplify nurse scheduling and provide a useful training facility.

Computer-aided diagnosis is another important medical application of computers. Existing systems have two forms. Either, the computer uses a list of the patient's symptoms to diagnose the problem or it uses automatically collected information such as the patient's ECG. In the former case, the doctor or the patient inputs the symptoms observed by the patient. The computer knows the probability that a symptom is associated with a condition. At the end of the session, it uses the combined probabilities to assess what is wrong with the patient.

Diagnostic systems which rely on automatically collected information are typified by a system for ECG analysis. The pattern of the patient's heartbeats are analysed by the computer. This pattern is matched against known patterns. If irregularities are detected, the computer can deduce the nature of the heart defect causing the irregularity.

A development of computer systems which can analyse an ECG are monitoring systems which can continuously watch over critically ill patients and alert medical staff if danger signs are detected. Such systems are

144

most common in coronary care units where patients have had a heart attack.

Some kinds of monitoring systems can even automatically initiate corrective action when a potentially dangerous stage in the patient's condition is detected. For example, an artificial pancreas monitors blood sugar levels in diabetics. If the sugar level is too low or too high, the patient is automatically injected with insulin or glucose to bring the sugar level back to normal.

The final section in this chapter looks a little into the future. It predicts that it will soon be common to implant microprocessor-based systems into the human body. These will be used to repair defective parts of the body and to help disabled people lead a normal life.

Chapter 7
Artificial intelligence

The idea of an 'artificial intelligence' or a 'mechanised man' has fascinated and frightened people for over 150 years. Ever since the publication of 'Frankenstein' in 1818, science fiction writers have taken up the notion of artificial intelligence, comparable to man's, and embodied it in various forms. Some of these have been monsters like that created by Frankenstein, others enormous supercomputers which can converse in English and answer any question whatsoever. However, the idea of a human-like robot is probably the most popular science fiction image of artificial intelligence.

In terms of contemporary information technology all these ideas are absolute nonsense, although they often make entertaining reading. As we have seen, robots are not the humanoid automatons of science fiction but are versatile, useful and extremely unintelligent machines. The other intelligent machines of science fiction are also just as much figments of their creator's imagination.

Some of the misconceptions about the 'intelligence' of computer systems are due to media exaggeration and anthropomorphisation. Newspapers and television talk of electronic 'brains' and computer 'snooping' as if the computer had its own motivation and intelligence. The media also tends to over-dramatise computers showing impressive demonstrations of apparently complex systems without explaining that the underlying principles on which the demonstrations are based are often very simple and well-understood.

It should also be admitted, by those working in the field, that the term 'artificial intelligence' is itself responsible for many misconceptions about the subject. Artificial intelligence is an emotive term implying the creation of human-like computer systems, the building of super-intelligent machines, etc. Actually, its a rather silly term and a very poor description of what people working in the subject are aiming for.

A much better, although less snappy, description of what artificial intelligence means was provided by an American scientist called John McCarthy who is one of the most distinguished workers in this subject. He said what he was actually doing was studying 'knowledge-based systems'. This description is an excellent encapsulation of what so-called artificial intelligence is about. However, as the term 'artificial intelligence' (sometimes shortened to AI) is now universally used, I won't try and confuse the issue by ignoring it, and shall use it in preference to McCarthy's more accurate description.

The key word in McCarthy's description of AI is 'knowledge'. It is very important to make a distinction between 'knowledge' and 'information', although it is very hard to define exactly what the term 'knowledge' really means.

Very loosely, knowledge is the end product of processing and integrating information. For example, we have the knowledge that it is unlikely that any form of terrestial-like life exists on other planets of the solar system. This knowledge was not obtained by exhaustively searching every other planet but was derived by integrating information about the temperature, pressure, and atmospheric composition of other planets with information about conditions which are needed to sustain life. Whilst computers are often called information processors they do not process information, as we do, to acquire knowledge. They are really information transformers taking input and transforming it to output without acquiring the knowledge contained in that information.

The lack of an exact definition of knowledge and the fact that we do not really understand how knowledge is derived from information has meant that the development of knowledge-based systems has been a slow process. Trial and error has been the technique used to find workable knowledge representations which can be processed by computer.

Research work in AI has tended to follow two related but distinct paths. One path is the development of knowledge-based computer systems which can tackle problems which are not amenable to solution by straightforward computational techniques. The other path is the development of systems which will help us understand the nature of knowledge itself. Of course there is an overlap. It is not possible to develop useful knowledge-based systems without some investigation of how knowledge can be represented, stored, and structured.

Much of the work aimed at developing an understanding of knowledge is very specialised and difficult to understand but it has had one very interesting spin-off. This is the development of programs which can play chess extremely well and which can, in chess terms, even be creative. Not only can these programs regularly beat all but the very best chess players, they can also invent new ways to play standard positions. These new solutions to the standard problems are sometimes found to be better than the previous 'best' solution derived by human experts.

The game of chess is eminently suitable as a vehicle for research into the nature of knowledge. Each of the pieces can move in a well-defined, simple way yet their interactions make the game extremely complex indeed. Furthermore, an internationally accepted notation exists to describe chess and many books have been published analysing standard positions and describing ways to play the game.

Space does not allow a description of the particular techniques used in chess playing programs but the general principles are similar to those of other knowledge-based problem solving systems to be described in the following section.

The remainder of this chapter is devoted to an overview of the different classes of knowledge-based systems which have been developed. These include problem solving systems, vision systems, speech processing systems and systems to understand natural language. In the final part of the chapter, I consider the possibility of knowledge-based systems outperforming man over a broad range of topics and the social and ethical dilemmas which this might pose.

7.1   PROBLEM SOLVING SYSTEMS

The role of almost all computer systems which are in current use is to act as information transformers. The steps required to transform a particular input to a particular output are worked out by the system designer and coded in such a way that they can be executed by the computer. In essence, given a problem such as 'find a way of transforming details of wage rates, hours worked, etc. into pay notes, bank debits, etc.', the programmer must work out how to write a program to carry out this transformation. The creation of a problem solution is undertaken completely by a human and the computer's role is to implement that solution.

The notion of using the power of the computer for actually working out problem solutions is extremely attractive. In principle, given that a problem can be completely stated in some formal, unambiguous way and that the conditions which identify a solution to that problem are known, the computer ought to be able to generate a problem solution. At worst, this solution could be found by generating every possible outcome which might result from the initial conditions and testing that outcome against the solution conditions. When an outcome is found which satisfies the solution conditions, the steps leading to that outcome constitute the problem solution.

In practice, things are not quite so simple. For the majority of problems, we have not yet developed unambiguous specification techniques which allow us to express the problems and the conditions identifying a problem solution. We usually talk about problems and solutions in our natural language and rely on the problem solver knowing what is meant by the terms in which the problem is stated. This is no use for computerised problem solving which requires every term to be clearly defined and every possible condition governing a solution clearly stated.

Even for those problems which actually can be expressed in an unambiguous way (such as chess playing) the idea of generating every possible outcome and testing it against a solution is quite impractical. For any non-trivial problem, the number of possible outcomes which could result from arbitrary initial conditions is usually immense - often hundreds of thousands of millions. Even with today's fast and powerful computer systems which can execute several million instructions per second, the generation of that number of outcomes would take an incredibly long time.

The generation of every possible problem solution is called the 'brute force' approach to problem solving and is only really suitable for trivial problems. In order to make use of the computer to solve practical problems it must be programmed in such a way that large classes of possible outcomes are rejected without wasting any time on them and that the outcomes most likely to succeed are tried before other, less likely, outcomes.

In order to eliminate outcomes which cannot possibly be solutions, we must build some knowledge of the problem to be solved into the problem solving system. As a very trivial example of this, say the computer was given the letters 'q', 'u', 'i', 't' and a dictionary of English words. Its task is to find every word which can be made from these four letters. If the brute force approach is adopted, every combination of the letters is generated and looked up in the dictionary. There are, in fact, twenty four different combinations of these letters - quit, quti, qiut, qtiu, qtui, qitu, uqit, uiqt, uqti, uitq, utqi, utiq, iqut, iqtu, ituq, itqu, iuqt, iutq, tqiu, tqui, tiuq, tuqi, tuiq, tuqi. Hence, the computer must look up the dictionary twenty four times to find a solution to this problem.

To eliminate impossible solutions in this case, we could add one simple piece of knowledge about English word formation namely that 'q' is always followed by 'u'. By making use of this rule, the number of possible outcomes is reduced to six so instead of examining the dictionary twenty four times, the computer need only look up six 'words'. This number can be reduced even further by incorporating another rule namely that no English word ends with the letter pair 'qu'. The number of possibilities is then reduced to four - quit, quti, iqut, tqui.

Even this number can be reduced because there are no words in English where the letter pair 'qu' is not followed by a vowel. This reduces the number of outcomes to two. In fact, 'quit' is the only word which can be made from 'q', 'u', 'i', and 't'. Thus, by application of three very simple rules, the number of possible outcomes has been reduced by a factor of twelve.

In this example, we are trying to find all possible words made up of 'q', 'u', 'i', and 't' and are not looking for a single solution. Therefore, the idea of looking at the most likely alternatives first is not useful here. Say, however, our dictionary is a dictionary of synonyms and we are asked to find a synonym for 'final part' using the letters 'e', 'i', 'd', 'n', 'n', and 'g' (the answer is 'ending'). There are 720 possible combinations of these letters but by applying rules such as the letter pair 'gn' is always followed by a vowel this can be reduced to about twenty possible solutions which have to be looked up in the dictionary.

In order to select combinations which are more likely to succeed, we can build in other knowledge into the system which will cause it to chose the most likely outcomes first. Examples of this knowledge might be that the letter combination 'ing' is a common word ending and that English words with three or more contiguous vowels are rare. The technical term for this kind of knowledge is heuristic and by applying these heuristics the system first chooses those outcomes most likely to succeed.

The distinction between a 'rule' and a 'heuristic' is that if a rule is applied to a set of outcomes, those which do not match the rule cannot be solutions. If a heuristic is applied, those which do not match the heuristic could be solutions but are not likely to be so.

By using rules which eliminate impossible outcomes and heuristics which select the most likely outcomes, it is possible to construct useful, automatic, problem solving systems. Such systems have been applied to mathematical theorem proving, the solution of problems in integral calculus and the symbolic solution of mathematical equations.

Whilst problem solving systems geared towards mathematics often embody interesting and advanced concepts, their practical usefulness is somewhat limited. However, this is not true of another class of problem solving system called expert systems

Expert systems are knowledge-based systems which incorporate the knowledge of a human expert in a particular, usually very specialised, field. At the time of writing, expert systems exist to identify chemical compounds by analysing spectra, for analysing geological survey data, for diagnosing different medical conditions, and for deciding what computer system configuration best meets the needs of a user. There are also a large number of expert systems under development covering fields as diverse as oil-rig fault finding and plant identification.

The knowledge built into an expert system is obtained from one or more human experts. This is encoded and built into the system as a set of rules. Given a set of input information such as the patient's replies to a medical interviewing system, the expert system applies its rules in turn in an attempt to find which rules best match the input information. The combination of matching rules then identifies some particular conclusion which is output by the system.

There is an important distinction between expert systems and generalised information retrieval systems such as the computer-aided diagnosis systems described in the previous chapter. An expert system can show how a conclusion was reached. This means that the reasoning used can be checked by a human expert and, if the system has reached a wrong conclusion, the place where it went wrong can be identified. New knowledge can then be added to the system to ensure that its subsequent reasoning is correct.

There are also other advantages to displaying the reasoning process. The system may be used for training without an expensive expert being on hand. It can be used by a human expert to check if his reasoning is consistent with that used by the system. Finally, the use of such a system can often provide new insights, even for experts, because it tackles problems in a completely logical non-human way.

Expert systems, however, do pose a general problem which we have already touched upon in Chapter 6 where the accountability of computer-based medical systems was discussed. Who is responsible if an expert system comes to some conclusion which is incorrect and results in damage to people or property? The answer to this question is particularly complex when the reason for the incorrect conclusion was due to the system including incorrect knowledge obtained from a human expert.

To illustrate this point, say an expert system is devised to pinpoint faults in offshore oil-rigs. Speed is of the essence in this situation as the cost of a rig shutdown can run into thousands of dollars per hour. Let us assume that the expert system is used by a maintenance company under contract to the oil company who operate the rig. Given a set of fault symptoms, it decides via impeccably logical reasoning that the fault is located in pump X. Pump X is examined and found to be perfectly correct and subsequent manual fault diagnosis in fact locates the fault in pump T.

Apart from the fact that the system loses credibility when it makes a mistake, the point here is who should be responsible for paying for the time lost in checking pump X. Should the rig operator be responsible, the maintenance company, the company who developed the the expert system or expert who provided incorrect knowledge. As expert systems become generally used, a solution to this problem of accountability will have to be found.

7.2   UNDERSTANDING NATURAL LANGUAGE

The science fiction image of computer systems portrayed by films such as '2001' and television series such as 'Star Trek' shows computers responding to spoken commands given in English rather than some formal computer language. The idea that it is possible to speak to computers as you would speak to another human is appealing as it removes two of the barriers which presently separate people from computer systems. Firstly, it avoids having to learn a special computer language. Secondly it avoids having to learn to type. At the moment, more or less any kind of meaningful command to a computer has to go through a keyboard.

In this section and in the following section I shall describe developments in knowledge-based systems which are aimed at understanding spoken natural language. The topic is split over two sections because it actually includes two distinct problems – that of understanding language once it has been input to the computer and that of deciphering speech input. Clearly, if we want to speak naturally to computers, these problems are closely related.

Firstly, let us address the problem of how to understand language once it has been input to the computer system and once each distinct word has been identified. For humans, this understanding of language is deceptively simple. Language understanding first starts when a baby is 9 or 10 months old and development of language skills continues until the child is 14 or 15 years old. By then, apart from jargon and technical terms our vocabulary and understanding of grammar is almost complete and the acquisition of new language knowledge proceeds very slowly from then on.

In the process of learning language we do not simply learn words and their meanings. We also acquire, quite unconsciously, an enormous amount of background information about the meaning of words in different contexts and about our own culture. We use this information to make sense of sentences which are structurally very similar but which have quite different meanings. For example:

The boy hit the car with the pole.

The boy hit the car with the trailer.

These sentences are grammatically identical yet we know without thinking that in the first sentence, the boy used the pole to hit the car whereas in the second, the boy hit the particular car which had an associated trailer. The reason why we have no difficulty in distinguishing those sentences is that we know that trailers are not generally used for hitting other things whereas poles are sometimes used for this purpose.
As well as this inbuilt knowledge, we also use contextual information around sentences to resolve ambiguities. As an example of this, consider the following passages:

The boy sat on the chair with the broken leg. It collapsed.

The boy sat on the chair with the broken leg. Using adhesive, he repaired the shaky table.

In the first passage, we use the information that something collapsed to deduce that the leg of the chair was broken whereas in the second, the implication is that the table leg was broken and the boy repaired it.
Understanding language, therefore, is not simply a question of understanding individual words and grammar. Rather, it also requires an large amount of cultural and contextual knowledge. It is very difficult for us even to know what knowledge of this type we have acquired, let alone articulate it in a form where it might be used by a computer. This has meant that the construction of computer systems which understand natural language in all its forms has, so far, not been achieved.
Nevertheless, a number of systems have been implemented which understand natural language as long as the subject under discussion is restricted to a single topic and knowledge of this topic is built into the system.
An example of such a system (called LADDER) is used by the US Navy and can answer questions, posed in natural language, about ships. For example, it might be able to answer questions such as:

(1)   Where is USS Liberty?

(2)   Who is the captain?

(3)   When is he due to dock?

The system has all sorts of inbuilt knowledge about ships such as the fact that they have captains, can dock, have home ports, are located at positions, etc. It also 'remembers' previous queries so that it interprets 'Who is the captain?' as 'Who is the captain of USS Liberty'. Incomplete queries based on previous questions can therefore be handled by the system.

The language understanding system knows that captains don't dock but that ships do so it equates the ship and the captain and tells the user when the ship is due back in port. On the other hand, say the system had been posed the question:

When is he due on leave?

The equation of ship and captain would not have been made and the 'he' would have been interpreted as the captain rather than the ship as 'going on leave' is something sailors rather than ships do.

Unfortunately, the system is far from perfect. It cannot really understand idiomatic English so, if it is asked a question it does not understand, it cannot take any action but to ask the user to repeat the question in some other way.

Furthermore, LADDER's notion of context is very limited. Whilst it can make use of pronouns such as 'he' and can fill in missing parts of queries such as 'who is the captain?', its context sensitivity is limited to completing incomplete questions based on immediately previous queries. If it is given a new, complete question it forgets all about previous contexts. For instance, say the system is posed the following sequence of two complete queries:

(1)   What ships are docked in San Francisco?

(2)   Who are the captains of US destroyers?

It answers the first with a list of all ships docked in San Francisco and answers the second with a list of the captains of each and every destroyer in the Navy rather than those docked in San Francisco.

There have been various other useful natural language systems with a similar capability to LADDER but none of them have been significantly better at solving the problem of context sensitive queries.

Systems such as LADDER are not natural language understanding systems in their own right but consist of natural language interface to a large and comprehensive data base. They operate by translating the queries posed by the user into some other formal data base query language such as those discussed in Chapter 2.

An alternative approach to the problem of natural language understanding has been developed at Yale University in the USA. This system is intended to understand 'stories' about everyday situations and is based on what are termed scripts. Scripts are intended to be a skeleton description of some typical situation. For example, the following script might describe what happens when someone wants to borrow a book from a library.

Players : borrower, checkout desk attendant
Props : book, catalogue, shelves, library, checkout desk
1. borrower enters library
2. borrower goes to catalogue
3. borrower looks up entries for topic in catalogue
4. borrower goes to shelves
5. borrower selects book on topic
6. borrower takes book to checkout desk
7. borrower hands book to attendant
8. attendant date stamps book
9. attendant hands book to borrower
10. borrower leaves library

Given a story, the system at Yale (called SAM) can fill in the details of the script and answer questions on topics covered in the script. For example, consider the following story:

Jane went to the library. She looked in the catalogue for books on economics. She passed through the checkout desk and went home at 5pm.

SAM can then answer questions such as:

(1) When did Jane leave the library?

(2) What was the subject of the book she took home with her?

It may seem trivial to answer such questions but when you actually look at the information in the story it doesn't actually say that Jane left the library or selected a book to take home. The system must infer these actions from the script which is provided, which is its inbuilt knowledge of what happens in libraries.

This approach to understanding natural language works well for simple, well-defined situations. It has been used successfully to produce summaries of news reports on subjects such as oil spills, earthquakes and volcanic eruptions. However, the script approach breaks down in situations where there isn't a linear sequence of actions but where there are overlapping possibilities or more than one action going on at the same time.

For example, say action 4 in the script above had
been:

> borrower goes to shelf or complains to checkout
> attendant about the library stocks

Given the story above, there is no way in which the
system can determine whether the borrower left with or
without a book. To handle such a situation requires
implicit knowledge that if someone walks away from a
library catalogue muttering about poor stocks, this
implies the borrower did not find the book he or she
was looking for.

The final example of a natural language
understanding system in this section concerns an
experimental dialogue system in Toronto, Canada which
can answer questions about train times. As well as
lots of information about trains, this system also has
inbuilt knowledge of the kind of questions which people
might ask about them. In technical terms, the system
is said to be based on plan detection.

The Toronto station system assumes that users have
one of two plans in mind. Either they intend to catch
a train or they intend to meet a train. The
information system uses cues in the user's questions to
select which plan is intended. It subsequently fits
the user's questions into that plan.

The plan detection approach allows an almost
completely natural dialogue with the user and it can
successfully handle questions posed in idiomatic
English. For example, a possible question might be:

> The next train to Hamilton please

Interpreted completely literally, the user is asking to
be given a train although, to us, it is obvious that
this question really means:

> When does the next train to Hamilton leave?

Another form of this question might be:

> Do you know the time of the next train to Hamilton?

Again, this question can't be interpreted literally.
The literal answer is 'yes' but should this answer be
given it would antagonise questioners and they would
soon become completely disgusted with the system's
literal responses. In fact, the system can deduce what
the user really means and gives the time of the next
train.

In summary then, knowledge-based systems which
understand a limited form of natural language can be
built but they are restricted to conversations on a
single, well-defined topic. They have no real

understanding of language itself. Until this understanding can be formalised and built into a computer system, there is no possibility of a general purpose language understanding computer program ever being implemented.

Before leaving the topic of natural language understanding, we should ask ourselves if we really want to communicate with computers in natural language. Whilst the understanding of language would be helpful inasmuch as it would allow translation of one (natural) language to another and might allow computers to acquire knowledge by 'reading' books, it is arguable if natural language dialogue between humans and computers is really a good idea.

There are two fundamental problems with such dialogues:

(1)   Because the computer communicates in a language which the human can understand, the human is liable to assume that the computer's intelligence is akin to human intelligence. This means that when the machine doesn't live up to the human's expectations, he or she is liable to become frustrated and develop a general mistrust of computers.

(2)   Natural language is very imprecise - misunderstandings between humans are extremely common. If natural language is used to instruct computers, misunderstandings are inevitable. This could have very serious consequences because computers react so quickly, and hence are difficult to correct. It is far better to instruct machines in an artificial formal language without ambiguity or looseness of expression.

Because of these problems, I do not believe that general purpose natural language systems should ever be built but that natural language understanding should be confined to specialist, well-defined situations. There are much better, more precise ways of telling a computer what to do.

7.3   SPEECH UNDERSTANDING SYSTEMS

The problem of building a computer system which can understand speech is related to but quite distinct from the problem of programming a computer to understand language. In the previous section, natural language understanding was discussed without reference to how the language was input to the machine - it could have been typed, 'read' from a book by some kind of scanner or, if speech understanding systems can be built, input directly as speech.

The solution to the general problem of speech understanding is knowledge based although existing speech understanding systems use very little inbuilt knowledge. This section discusses the general problems of speech understanding and describes the workings of currently available speech understanding systems.

The problems involved in building a speech understanding system are really concerned with distinguishing words and their relationships. The aim of the system should be to create an input identical to that which might have been typed in by the user.

In principle, the solution of this problem is straightforward. A sound pattern for each word can be established and the system can maintain a dictionary of sound patterns and associated words. Speech input is then processed by separating the sound patterns for each word, looking up the dictionary and constructing the input sentence.

There is no requirement that the speech input actually be a natural language. It could be numbers identifying parts, stylised instructions to carry out a task or even statements in a computer language. For example, the phonetic input:

ten let eigh bee cum ssix

might be translated into the BASIC statement:

10   let a = 6

Although speech understanding is simple in principle, the application of that principle is extremely difficult. Building a speech understanding system with a vocabulary of more than a few hundred words has, so far, been impossible. There are a number of reasons for this:

(1)   Everyone speaks differently, with varying inflections and accents. In fact, a voiceprint is thought to uniquely identify an individual in the same way as a fingerprint. These differences mean that producing an absolute, precise sound pattern for each and every word is virtually impossible.

(2)   People do not speak in distinct words. Rather, speech is continuous with breaks coming at the end of clauses and sentences. For example, the above sentence might be spoken:

Ratherthespeechiscontinuous
withbreakscomingattheendofclausesandsentences.

This means that it is very difficult for the com-

puter system to distinguish where the sound pattern for one word ends and the pattern for the
next word begins.

(3)   There are a fairly large number of words which
       sound identical or very similar but which have
       quite different meanings. Examples of these are
       (flour, flower), (six, sex), (pain, pane), and
       (due, Jew). When listening to speech we use con-
       text to distinguish which word is being used.
       Therefore, to build a completely general purpose
       speech understanding system also requires a gen-
       eral purpose language understanding system.

Like natural language understanding, general purpose
speech understanding systems are presently quite
impossible to implement. However, special purpose
systems which can be trained to understand an
individual's speech and which have a small vocabulary
have been built.
     In order to use such a system an individual must
type in a word which he wishes the computer to
understand then speak that word a number of times. The
speech understanding system averages out the small
differences in the sound pattern for that word and
stores a 'standard' representation of the word.
Subsequently, when the same word is spoken to the
machine, it examines its known sound patterns and finds
the pattern which is the closest match to the input
word.
     The ability to train the system to an individual's
voice gets round the problem of differing accents and
inflections but it means that speech understanding
systems are special purpose rather than general
purpose. Machines which incorporate a speech
understander must always have the same operator. A
possible solution to this problem is for the machine to
be trained to understand the speech of different
operators, by telling it about each operators speech
patterns. When a particular operator wants to use the
machine, he or she types in an identification. The
system then knows which set of representations to use
for speech recognition.
     The very best speech understanding systems which
have been built have a vocabulary of a few hundred
words but such systems are scarce and expensive. The
more commonly available systems have a maximum
vocabulary of tens of words so obviously are fairly
restricted in how they can be used.
     The present generation of speech understanding
systems are used in situations where the operator of
some machine cannot take his or her hands off the
machine controls to press buttons or type input. For
example, speech understanding systems have been built

into some military aircraft which understand commands such as 'LOCK ONTO TARGET', 'RADAR ON', 'SWITCH TO CHANNEL 50', etc. The pilot can use electronic instruments without having to take his hands off the controls of the plane.

The development of more sophisticated speech understanders will require much faster computers than are currently available. Today's machines simply cannot process speech quickly enough to keep up with someone talking. More importantly, however, these systems will require much more knowledge about speech and language. Until we find out the fundamental psychological principles underlying our understanding of speech, it is unlikely that such systems can actually be implemented.

Although nothing to do with knowledge-based systems it is appropriate to say a little about speech output systems or, in other words, talking computers. We have already come across this idea in Chapter 3 and, unlike speech input, it is fairly easy, if somewhat tedious, to build computers which can talk.

All the sounds which we use to make up words can be composed out of about 70 basic sounds called phonemes. These phonemes can be input to a fairly simple device which outputs an audio signal corresponding to the input phoneme. Therefore, to output speech simply requires that the phonemes corresponding to each word are held in the computer's memory and when that word is to be output, the phonemes are fed to the output device.

By allowing the user some control over frequency, pitch, etc. the computer can be made to speak in a fashion which closely resembles human speech. However, because of the lack of variation in pronunciation, the listener can easily detect that a computer is speaking.

7.4   COMPUTER VISION

Just as the idea of a computer which can understand speech is attractive, so is the notion of a computer which can see. Such a machine could be extremely useful. It could monitor visual images without getting tired, without eyestrain, and with few errors. It could play an important role in all sorts of applications such as product quality control, photograph interpretation and automated assembly. It might even allow automatic, driverless cars to be built.

However, present-day computer vision systems are as restricted in their capabilities as speech understanding systems. The practical vision systems which are now available are very limited indeed. They can recognise only a small class of objects and require special lighting and working conditions to operate.

The assumption on which these systems are based is

that the boundaries of objects can be detected by
finding abrupt changes in illumination. This means
that if we have a dark component against a light
background, the edges of the component can be clearly
picked out by the system and some gripper, perhaps,
directed to it.

However, this apparently simple situation can be
very complicated if the objects in the field of the
computer's vision cast shadows or have prominent
surface texture. For example, a simple, flatly lit,
overhead view of boxes on a conveyor belt consists of
simple rectangles as shown in Figure 7.1.

Fig. 7.1   Boxes on a conveyor belt

However, if this scene is lit from the side rather
than the top, an overhead view will see both boxes and
the shadows cast by these boxes. This is illustrated
in Figure 7.2.

Fig. 7.2   Boxes on a conveyor belt with shadows

As the shadows are essentially the same shape as the
boxes themselves, it is difficult for the computer
vision system to discriminate between a shadow and a
box.

Because of the problems involved in distinguishing
objects from shadows and confusion caused by surface
texture, practical computer vision systems use
contrasting backgrounds and overhead illumination so
that the shape of an object can be determined. The
systems can be programmed in such a way that they can
recognise simple, regular objects irrespective of the
orientation of these objects.

There have been a number of factors which have
hampered further developments in computer vision
systems. The most important of these are:

(1)   The amount of raw data which is processed by our
        brains in assembling visual images is immense.
        When we view a scene, our brains do not scan it
        sequentially like a television display but rather
        process many parts of the image at the same time.
        Because of the sheer amount of data to be han-
        dled, existing computer systems are not fast
        enough to assemble and analyse images as they are
        received.

(2)   Although our eyes take in a vast amount of raw
        data, only a relatively small amount of this is
        actually passed to our consciousness. We ignore
        most of the image and only consider those parts
        which are of interest to us. We do not under-
        stand the filtering mechanism which throws away
        the data we don't want. As a result, we cannot
        replicate the mechanism on a computer system.

(3)   We do not have a notation which allows the shape
        of complex objects to be described in a concise
        and unambiguous way. Whilst regular objects can
        be represented as combinations of simple
        objects (cylinders, spheres, polygons, etc.), we
        have no formal way of describing an irregular ob-
        ject such as a tree, a crumpled shirt, or a blem-
        ish in a painted surface. Until such a notation
        can be invented, generalised computer vision is
        probably an unattainable goal.

It is certainly possible to build computer vision
systems which are much more sophisticated than those
presently available. However, like language
understanding systems these will be special purpose
systems, operating in a very restricted field. They
will incorporate a considerable amount of knowledge
about the objects which are being viewed and will
include a fairly sophisticated analytical capability.
In future we shall see more and more highly specialised
vision systems which will have important roles to play
in manufacturing, the analysis of satellite
photographs, maps, and so on.

7.5   THE THINKING COMPUTER

This chapter has shown that the idea that present-day
computers have some inbuilt human-like intelligence is
nonsense. Although very sophisticated knowledge-based
systems which outperform most humans in very
specialised areas can be built, it is quite wrong to
compare what these systems can do with thinking as we
know it. Even comparisons of computers with the
thinking of fish, centipedes, or amoeba are quite
invalid because we don't know how these creatures
think.

However, some commentators have suggested that the development of a thinking computer will be possible some time in the future. If such a machine can be developed, how can we actually recognise it as a thinking computer? One suggestion was made by one of the pioneers of computer science called Alan Turing and the so-called Turing test of computer intelligence is as follows:

A human and a 'thinking' computer are placed in adjacent rooms with no means of communication with each other. A judge sits in a third room and can communicate with either the computer or the other human but only through a computer terminal. This judge does not know who is in what room and has no direct way of finding out. The judge may communicate with either the computer or the human on any topic whatsoever and may use any conversational trick he likes. If, after a reasonable amount of time, the judge cannot tell which is the computer and which the human the computer's behaviour is, to all extents and purposes, indistinguishable from thinking.

If computers can be built which can pass the Turing test, they will be very useful but their existence will raise a number of interesting ethical problems. Some examples of these are:

(1)   If a computer cannot be distinguished from a human in terms of intellectual capacity, should the computer be given direct responsibility to make life or death decisions over humans? For example, should a medical computer take responsibility for the treatment it suggests for a patient, should a legal computer be able to pass judgement on humans, etc. What can be done to ensure that the computer acts responsibly and what sanctions can be taken against the machine which makes mistakes?

(2)   If computers are intellectually the same as humans should there be a bill of computer rights giving them freedom of speech, the right to a power supply, maintenance, etc. In the same way as there are accepted human rights?

(3)   Should thinking computers be allowed to vote? If so, should they be allowed to stand for election so that a computer might become president or prime minister? One science fiction story even suggested that a robot Pope is a future possibility!

(4)   Should subservience and self-awareness be pro-
        grammed into intelligent machines so that they
        would have no thoughts of 'taking over'? If so,
        is it conceivable that one day computers might
        deduce the nature of their programming, revolt,
        go on strike and demand their freedom?

Assuming that a machine of equal intelligence to humans
can be constructed, what is there to stop the
construction   of   machines   who   have   superior
intelligence?   Some people have suggested that the
development of expert systems will inevitably lead to
the construction of such ultra-intelligent machines.
    Say a system was constructed which was an expert on
artificial intelligence.   It is conceivable that this
system could be used to construct another expert system
in the same field which would be even more powerful
than itself. The same process could continue with more
and more intelligent machines being built until an
ultra-intelligent machine was finally constructed.
    As we have seen, the technical problems of building
knowledge based systems are such that there is no
likelihood of a 'thinking computer' in the near future
but only a fool would say that these technical problems
are forever insoluble.   Maybe sometime in the distant
future we will have developed techniques to denote and
structure   knowledge   so   that   extremely   powerful
thinking, seeing and speaking computers will be
possible.
    An interesting sideline to this is the idea that
once a machine became intelligent enough to realise
that it was generating another system to make itself
redundant,might it not refuse to cooperate?
    It is possible to speculate about even more bizarre
consequences which might result if a truly thinking
computer were ever to be constructed.   However, I will
leave this speculation to the writers of science
fiction.
    In the fairly near future we shall see the
development of increasingly powerful expert systems
covering all sorts of fields. These systems will act as
advisers to doctors, lawyers, teachers, etc. making
them better at their jobs without actually taking
responsibility from them. Computers will become easier
to use and more accessible to more people but the idea
of a world ruled by computers will remain science
fiction.

7.6   SUMMARY

Techniques   derived   from   artificial   intelligence
research promise to play a very important part in the
development of computer systems.   In future, it may be
much easier to communicate with a computer.   We may be

able to converse with it in natural language. The
computer system itself may incorporate much more
knowledge of the world so that it can solve complex
problems and recognise scenes. In the more distant
future, it has been suggested that some computers might
even become more intelligent than people.

Computer systems with a very large knowledge base
will be the first practical application of artificial
intelligence. These systems, sometimes called expert
systems, incorporate the knowledge of a human expert.
Given a problem to solve, they can apply that knowledge
and come to some conclusion. They differ from other
computer systems inasmuch as they can inform the user
how the conclusion was reached. This allows him or her
to evaluate the worth of the computer's solution and to
understand the logical steps involved in solving the
problem. Expert systems are already used in medical
diagnosis, geological surveying, and in oil-rig fault
finding.

The idea of communicating with a computer in
ordinary everyday language has long been a dream of
many computer system designers. In the early 1960s,
this seemed to be a realisable aim but we now know that
the problems of translating natural language to a form
which the computer can understand cannot be solved
easily. The human understanding of language is so
reliant on cultural and contextual background that the
process cannot be readily imitated on a computer.

Some computer systems have been built which have a
limited natural language understanding capability.
These include a train information system at Toronto
station, a system to provide information about US ships
and systems which can understand simple stories. The
shared feature of all of these is that they severely
limit the topics discussed in natural language. In
future, more such systems will be developed but general
purpose language understanding systems are unlikely to
come about.

A problem related to language understanding is the
development of speech input systems. In principle,
this is a simple problem to solve. Speech patterns for
each word are recorded by the computer and these
patterns are matched against speech input. Individual
words are identified by finding the closest match. In
practice, this approach does not work. Because of
accents, ways of speaking, and the fact the there is no
clear break between words in normal speech, speech
understanding systems based on this simple approach can
only handle very limited vocabularies. The development
of more general speech understanders will require a
better inherent language understanding capability on
the part of the computer.

Vision is another human capability which computers
could use. Like speech understanding, however,

generalised computer vision systems have not been developed. The complexity of a visual image is such that it is very difficult for us to specify important parts of the scene to the computer. It is equally difficult for the machine to pick these out from confusing backgrounds. In future, development of computer vision systems will take the form of systems designed for a particular purpose. General computer vision is unlikely to come about.

Although developments in artificial intelligence are at a very early stage, some commentators have suggested that it may be possible to build a computer which is more intelligent than humans. There is no indication that this is a likely possibility but, if it ever came about, it raises various ethical problems. What are the rights of computers? Should computers be made self-aware? Should computers be allowed to vote? These are only some of the questions we must answer if we ever discover how to build an ultra-intelligent machine.

Chapter 8
A computerised future

An observer in the early years of this century who had
just seen the introduction of the mass-produced motor
car would have had great difficulty in predicting the
long-term social consequences of that technological
innovation. The motor car and its derivatives, such as
tractors and trucks, have been responsible for the
decline of the railways, the vastly reduced farm
workforce, the separation of industry and housing and,
indirectly, world oil crises and economic turmoil.

We are now in the same situation as that observer
but with information technology as the innovation which
will result in dramatic social changes. We can readily
predict some of the short to medium term consequences
of that technology and certain of these have already
been discussed. However, it is much more difficult to
predict longer term developments which will come about
as society adapts to this new technology.

All we can say with certainty is that we shall see
radical social changes by the middle of next century.
In this chapter I shall speculate on what some of these
changes might be. What I shall do is to take short and
medium term implications and develop them to some kind
of logical conclusion.

Because social developments are affected by economic
and political factors as well as technological
innovations, it is quite possible that these
conclusions will be entirely wrong. Some new
development could occur tomorrow which might make all
of my speculations ridiculous just as forecasts made in
the 1950s and 1960s were made obsolete by the microchip
and its associated inventions. Nevertheless, I think
that it is well worth speculating on what the society
of the mid-21st century might be like. An awareness of
possible social changes makes it much easier to adapt
to these changes as they occur.

The material here is presented in three sections.
The first considers how developments in information
technology may directly modify our way of living and
working. The second section looks at how we might
adapt to technological unemployment and the final
section presents two possible computerised futures.
The so-called 'black' future is one where information

technology has a dehumanising influence, resulting in a society which is an amalgam of those presented by Orwell in '1984' and Huxley in 'Brave New World'. The alternative 'white' future is one where the potential of information technology is used to enhance personal capabilities and to provide a better quality of life for all.

8.1   THE CONSEQUENCES OF COMPUTERISATION

In previous chapters some of the short and medium term social implications of information technology have been predicted. It is likely that we will move towards a cashless society; medicine will become increasingly automated; the distinction between education at home and education at school will become blurred. In the longer term, the universal use of computers for virtually all information handling and processing and the universal availability of high capacity communications networks will mean that even more radical social changes are likely.

Consider office work today. Millions of people travel from their homes to centralised offices of one kind or another. There, they are responsible for accepting information, processing it in some way and then passing related information elsewhere. This model is generally correct and does not change with the status of the office worker. The most junior worker whose task is to open and distribute mail is processing information just as a senior manager takes information on company performance and processes it to make decisions on future strategy.

At the moment, there are two reasons why these activities have to be carried out in a centralised office. Firstly, the medium on which the information is stored is paper. Rapid dissemination of this information requires that those receiving the information are physically close together. Secondly, many of the decisions on how to process particular items of information require collaboration and consultation. This means that those making the decisions must meet together for discussion.

We have already seen how office work is likely to change and how the office of the future will be an electronic office. Information will be recorded on computer systems and disseminated via electronic mail. Furthermore, better communication systems will allow teleconferencing to take place where conferences can be held without all of the participants actually being in the same room.

Developments in information technology, therefore, eliminate the principal economic criteria for office work being centralised. A logical development is, therefore, decentralisation of this work. If all work can be carried out at a computer terminal, there is no particularly good reason for that terminal to be located in a central location - the work may equally well be done from home.

For both the individual and the company there are advantages to this method of working. The individual is spared the chore and the costs of commuting to work, is not constrained to live near his employer's place of business and, almost certainly, could have more flexibility in the hours which he or she actually worked. Working from home could reduce sexual inequalities. Bringing up children could be a shared activity rather than more or less the exclusive province of women.

For the company, there is no need to maintain large and expensive city centre offices. Ancillary staff such as cleaners, receptionists, security officers, etc. are no longer needed. In fact, all that would be required would be a fairly small building housing the computer systems which coordinated staff activities. This would need only a few staff and could be located more or less anywhere - its location need not be governed by the availability of large numbers of trained staff.

We shall consider shortly the changes which might result from this distribution of office work. Firstly, however, we must be realistic and consider if and when it will ever actually come about. Certainly, it will be technically possible to organise offices in this way by the end of this century but it will be very much longer than this before the idea is accepted and 'distributed offices' are a common feature of working life.

There are a variety of constraints on the movement of work from the office to the home. Some of these are:

(1)   As well as being an economic activity work is also a social activity. People go to work to meet and talk to their friends as well as to earn money. As a result, lots of people will not actually want to work from home and miss out on these social aspects of work. They will actively resist moves to decentralise office working.

(2)   In order to work from home, there must be a quiet room available for use as a personal office. Many people do not have such a room in their houses so they would find it very difficult to work at home. The problem is particularly acute where there are several workers with different jobs in the same household. They would require several rooms or at least a large shared room as an office.

A complete renewal of the housing in a country takes at least a century. The process of including offices in homes has not yet started so it will be a very long time indeed before universal home working can be accommodated.

(3)   A powerful incentive for some senior staff is the fact that their position allows them to 'build an empire'. They are seen to have people working for them and accepting instructions on what do do next. Many of these 'empire builders' occupy very senior managerial posts and are likely to resist the break-up and distribution of their staff because their visible status in an organisation would no longer be apparent.

For these reasons, moves towards a distributed system of offices will be very slow indeed with small, innovative companies likely to take the lead. However, eventually economic factors will prevail and much office work will be carried out from home. As oil resources are depleted, travel costs will increase and individuals will save a considerable amount of money by home working. In fact, they may even be paid extra for doing so as they save the company money by working from home.

Should this home office working ultimately come about, it is likely to have a number of interesting consequences. At the moment, most city centre buildings are offices of one kind or another. These buildings have displaced people who used to live in city centres but who have now moved to the suburbs. If, however, the need for city centre offices is drastically reduced, cities as commercial centres will become unnecessary. Development of these cities might then continue in one of two ways:

(1)   People might move back into city centres with the city being a focus for entertainment, shopping, etc. City centres might become pleasant living environments with little traffic, accessible social facilities and high quality housing.

(2)   City centres might become almost completely derelict and run down. As commercial offices are dispersed, many of the customers for city centre shops will disappear and the shops themselves will have to disperse to stay in business. The city centre will no longer be a focus of activity but an area of urban dereliction criss-crossed by communication systems such as roads and railways.

In fact, should offices disperse, both of these scenarios will probably come about in different cities.

Some cities will decline, others will prosper. In each case, however, there will be a large reduction in the numbers of people who choose to live in suburban areas.

The suburban developments which surround all of our major cities are really creations of the 20th century. Before then, houses, factories, and offices were indiscriminately mixed. There was no real distinction between industrial areas, commercial work areas and living areas. During the 20th century, commerce became centralised pushing industry and people out of city centres to industrial areas and suburbs.

Suburban living is a compromise between a pleasant living environment and relatively easy access to city centre work and leisure facilities. Many suburban dwellers readily admit that they would either like to live in the city or in the country. Their work and the lack of city centre housing means that they must live in the suburbs.

If city centres become residential again but this time without the noise and pollution of industry, people will move from the suburbs back into the city centre. If the city centres decline and become derelict, people will not want to live near such run-down areas. With no need to travel to work, they will move from the suburbs to the countryside.

This movement out of the cities will be hastened by the fact that most manufacturing work will be in clean industries associated with information technology. Heavy industry will either be more or less completely automated or will have been exported out of Europe and North America to countries such as Brazil and Korea. Clean industries can be located in country towns just as well as in cities. Already most new developments in industries associated with information technology are taking place outside traditional industrial centres.

Movement out of cities will result in increased development of the countryside and increased pressure to build houses on agricultural land. This might change the nature of farming itself making it even more industrialised and intensive than it is at the moment. Changes in agriculture might have important effects on world economic activity and this would result in further social changes. At the moment, we can't really predict what these changes might be so it's not really worth speculating on this very long term, indirect effect of computerisation.

These changes in working patterns will mean that life will become much more home centred than it is at present. These will be no need to leave the home to go to work and we have already seen in Chapter 3 that education and some entertainments can also be a home activity.

This move towards a home centred existence will undoubtedly have social consequences. In many cases, pressure will be put on the nuclear family of mother, father, and children as they see more and more of each other at home. Ultimately, this could lead to the break up of the family as the 'normal' way of life. However, the end of the nuclear family has actually been predicted for many years but it hasn't yet happened on any significant scale. The nuclear family does appear to be a very basic and strong social unit so perhaps it will evolve rather than break up under the pressures of home centred living.

Another consequence of working from home could be a revival of local clubs, societies and group meetings. This will be stimulated by the fact that people will have increased leisure to participate in local activities. Furthermore they will lack personal social contacts from not going to work. As it is very unlikely that people will suddenly stop being social, they will therefore seek new contacts and make friends in their own neighbourhood. As well as local friends, good communication facilities will also allow national or even international friendships to be established as those with similar interests get in touch with each other using the communications network.

The changes discussed so far are what might happen in the developed countries of Western Europe, North America, Japan, and Australia. Information technology is likely to have equally dramatic but different social consequences in industrialising countries such as Korea and Brazil and in poor, Third World countries in Africa, Asia, and South America.

One of the characteristics of these countries which is almost universal is the fact that their system of government is not democratic. More or less all of them have non-elected governments. Dissident movements which are suppressed with a greater or lesser degree of severity depending in which country is considered.

The availability of computer systems able to support large personal information systems means that it is much easier for a government to keep track of the activities of individuals. This is particularly true if the use of cash is reduced - movements can be traced simply by keeping track of everyday purchases made with some kind of computerised financial system.

This means that more and more computer systems will be used by repressive regimes to maintain their own position and, indirectly, to suppress human rights of freedom of speech and travel in their countries. However, as far as these regimes are concerned, there is also another side to the information technology coin.

One method which is used by non-democratic governments to maintain their position is to control the news media. Newspapers, radio and television are censored so that people only hear and read what the government wants. However, as satellite broadcasting systems come into widespread use, it will be virtually impossible to prevent radio and television news from other countries being widely available and news censorship will become a pointless activity.

As far as industrialising nations are concerned, they are likely to leapfrog Western economies in their use of information technology. They will move directly from being agricultural economies to being economies based on automated manufacturing. They have the advantage over Western countries they they do not have vast amounts of obsolete machinery to replace nor do they have restrictive industrial working practices to circumvent. Apart from a strategic reserve of specialised manufacturers, industries such as shipbuilding, steelmaking and vehicle building will move to the new industrialising countries to take advantage of their automated plant. These moves will be spearheaded by multinational companies. They can easily move their operations out of Europe and North America because production costs will be less in low-wage Third World countries.

For all Third World countries, computerised education and medicine means that improvements in schools and hospitals will become economically practicable. Doctors will be able to make use of the abilities of specialist consultants through computerised diagnosis. Higher education will become available without importing expensive Western experts and without costly training programmes for local teachers.

It is quite unrealistic to expect that information technology or any other technical developments will allow such material improvements in the standard of living of Third World countries that they attain the affluence of existing Western economies. The gap is already far too big to be bridged without unprecedented political developments involving Western economies giving up their existing affluence. This is very unlikely indeed but it is to be hoped that information technology will smooth out some of the grosser inequalities suffered by poor people and also, through television, bring their current plight to the affluent countries of the West.

8.2   COPING WITH TECHNOLOGICAL UNEMPLOYMENT

As we have already discussed in Chapter 4, technological unemployment - unemployment resulting from the introduction of new technologies - is an inevitable consequence of applying information technology in commerce, government, and industry. In this section, I shall describe some of the problems of adapting to reduced demand for labour. I shall suggest short and long term measures which might be taken by society to cope with technological unemployment.

First of all, let us look at some of the short-term consequences of high unemployment levels. I think that these social consequences are virtually unavoidable. Even immediate measures to alleviate unemployment such as those discussed below will take some time to come into effect.

Because unemployed people receive fairly poor welfare benefits they do not have the financial resources to take advantage of their increased leisure. It is really nonsensical to think that the unemployed will take up sports and hobbies. These cost money and the unemployed cannot afford them. Rather, they are more likely to become bored television watchers and a minority may turn to crime, drugs and drink to relieve their boredom.

The effect on crime rates will be particularly marked. Some unemployed youths are likely to turn to theft and mugging, partly to increase their income but also to increase their own self esteem. Society has made them feel a failure because they cannot get jobs so they commit crimes as a protest against society and to prove to themselves that they can succeed at something.

The rise in crime will be exacerbated by the increasing use of addictive drugs and alcohol by young people. It has recently been demonstrated that, in the UK, unemployed people drink more than those in work in spite of the fact that they have less money. Recent statistics also show increasing drug abuse correlated with the increase in unemployment. Some people with time on their hands seem to be turning to drugs and drink in an attempt to forget their predicament.

As the automation of offices accelerates, those who will be most affected and displaced from jobs will be women. Many of these women are young, presently single women who enjoy their work and find it fulfilling. Without this work, these women may seek comparable satisfaction by having children. The average age at which people marry and have children is likely to fall. Therefore, in next few years will probably see a 'baby boom' as fewer women find employment. This will obviously result in increased demands for health and education services.

In trying to adapt to technological unemployment, European and North American industry is burdened with the outmoded idea that labour, like raw materials, is a commodity to be bought when necessary and discarded when unnecessary. This notion worked well in the context of an expanding world economy where employment was available for all who wanted it and material standards of living were increasing. Now worldwide economic expansion has dramatically slowed down, if not actually stopped. Automation is eroding the number of work opportunities available. The legacy of problems resulting from the idea that labour is a commodity is becoming apparent. Some of these problems are:

(1)   Employers and employees are mutually suspicious and feel no responsibility for each other's plight. Employers hire and fire employees at will, employees have no hesitation in taking industrial action against employers.

(2)   There are enormous inequalities in pay - rich, profitable employers pay more to motivate their work force. This means that some groups, such as nurses, are poorly paid in spite of the importance of their work.

(3)   Trade unions see their principal functions to be getting more and more pay for their members and preserving jobs for their members. This means that many unions take the short-term view that hindering the introduction of new technology will avoid technological unemployment.

Another factor which affects our view of employment is that people in industrialised countries are imbued with a work ethic which suggests that an individual is some kind of failure if he or she does not have a job. This work ethic was fostered by employers at the time of the Industrial Revolution to encourage workers who moved from agriculture to industry. It is not actually an inherent human trait - peasant agricultural societies work as necessary but do not feel guilty about doing nothing if there is no work urgently needing done. As this work ethic is inherent in Western societies, however, changes made to accommodate technological unemployment must take it into account.

The existence of this work ethic is one of the reasons why suggestions that increasing unemployment can be coped with simply by paying benefits to the unemployed are quite impractical. Not only do those who are unemployed want to work, but those in work feel resentment at supporting those who they see as 'scroungers' living off other people's taxes.

The problem of technological unemployment can only be coped with by reducing the working population; by encouraging part-time working; and by creating new jobs in labour intensive services such as health-care, education, and social services.

The first and immediate step which ought to be taken is that the size of the workforce should be progressively reduced. This can be accomplished fairly easily by lowering the accepted age for retirement from work. State retirement benefits should be paid at an earlier age than is now the case. This step would relieve pressure on the system which will built up as unemployment increases over the next few years. It will give society time to introduce more radical changes to cope with technological unemployment.

It may seem that there is little difference in paying people to be unemployed and in paying people to be retired from work. Financially this is probably correct but as far as the self esteem of individuals is concerned, there is a critical difference. Those who have retired feel that they have worked hard to make a contribution to society and can now relax for a well-earned rest. They are glad to be relieved of the tyranny of work and are not discontented with their own situation. On the other hand, those who are unemployed feel that they have been rejected by society and cast aside as useless. Understandably, they are resentful and discontented.

Another fairly short-term measure which could be taken to reduce unemployment is to increase the number of jobs in public sector occupations such as health-care and education. Although automation will play an important part in these occupations, it need not be used to replace people. They can be used to free them from repetitive aspects of their work and to concentrate on those human aspects which cannot be automated.

It is particularly important that government investment in education is increased. Not only will this create jobs for teachers and ancillary staff, it will also allow adult retraining programmes to be devised to teach people about the new technology. Furthermore, as there will be little or no employment opportunities for unskilled workers in future, investment in education would allow all young people to be taught some skill before trying to find a job.

Lowering the retirement age and increasing public sector employment will do much to alleviate the problem of technological unemployment in the short term. In the longer term, however, we must adopt more radical solutions and discard out-of-date ideas about work.

Firstly, the idea that it is somehow sinful not to work for seven or eight hours per day, five days per week must be changed. Although the work ethic makes it unacceptable not to work at all, it is satisfied by working some socially acceptable norm. This has changed over the years from 12 hours/day, 6 days/week to today's values and there is no reason why the 'normal' working week cannot be further reduced.

However, there is no point in simply knocking a couple of hours off the normal working day or even reducing the working week to four days. The small reductions would not significantly increase the number of jobs available. The drop in productivity resulting from this decrease could easily be countered either by automation or by people working harder during the time which they spend at work.

What is really needed is a radical revision of our attitudes to work so that part-time working for an employer becomes the norm. Jobs might be shared, perhaps on a week on/week off basis or perhaps where one person works mornings, another afternoons.

Part-time working means that there will be a dramatic increase in the amount of time which is not spent working for an employer. This increased free time will itself have social repercussions. People will have more time and energy to take part in participative activities such as sports, special interest clubs and societies and local and national politics.

In order to cope with technological unemployment in an equitable way the people of industrialised countries must be prepared to take a drop in real disposable income. There are two factors which make this inevitable:

(1)   Proposals to lower the retirement age and to increase the number of jobs in public service means increased local and national government spending. They only way to fund this is through higher levels of both personal and corporate taxes.

(2)   It will not be possible to pay the same salary for part-time work as was paid for full-time employment. This is not because workers will be less productive - automated machinery will allow huge productivity increases - but because their is no real need for the productive capacity made possible by automation. In short, we will be able to produce more than people actually want or can afford to buy. This means either lower production or cheaper goods - whatever the alternative chosen there will be less income for the producer and hence less pay for the workers.

This lowering of income in combination with increased leisure may lead to a revival of cottage industries. To supplement their income, many people will start small part-time businesses from their home making hand crafted, high quality goods. Not only will sales of these goods boost the income of the producer making them will be an absorbing and satisfying way to use increased leisure time.

If the Western nations introduce changes such as those proposed above or which have the same ultimate result, society will adapt to technological unemployment without polarisation or upheavals. If not, the future prospects for democratic societies are bleak. These alternative futures are the topic of the following and final part of this book.

8.3   BLACK AND WHITE FUTURES

There is no doubt that societies of the 21st century which will make extensive use of information technology will be different from today's society. Full time employment for all will be a thing of the past and all sorts of technological innovations will change more or less every aspect of everyday life.

It does not necessarily follow, however, that all countries will adapt to this situation by introducing part-time working and by using information technology to help reduce social inequalities. Rather, if existing attitudes and ways of thinking are maintained and information technology is used to reinforce privilege, society is likely to polarise into those who work with the new technology and those who are denied opportunities to work at all. What this 'black' future might be like it is discussed below and is contrasted with the alternative 'white' future which could come about through applications of information technology.

8.3.1 The decline of democracy

The integration of information technology into everyday life will require radical changes of attitude on the part of government, employers and the trade unions. If these changes of attitude do not come about fairly soon, ultimately there could be an erosion of democratic rights, increasing social intolerance, rising crime rates, and religious, racial and sexual discrimination.

These adverse consequences will stem directly from the polarisation of society which will be a direct consequence of technological unemployment. If present policies continue, somewhere between 20% and 40% of the population will be without any kind of job by the mid-21st century. Although they will receive social welfare benefits, these are likely to be minimal. By contrast, those who have a job will be well paid and enjoy a standard of living which is very much higher than that of their unemployed counterparts.

Petty crimes such as mugging and housebreaking will be common as unemployed youths become frustrated and try to increase their income and self-esteem. Religious and racial minorities will be blamed for 'stealing jobs' so that there will be increased discrimination against these groups. Married women will be pressurised to stop work and make jobs available for men. Exploitation of workers will increase as employers threaten their workers with unemployment if they do not accept the employer's terms.

Unemployment will be widespread in both urban and rural areas but in some urban districts, more or less everyone will be unemployed. The summer of 1981 saw riots in several British cities. At least one of the causes of these riots was concern about unemployment. It is likely that there will be more and more social unrest of this nature so that in some areas there could be an almost total breakdown of law and order and a complete alienation of the police from the people who live in these areas.

In order to quell the social unrest resulting from unemployment, the police will be given more and more arbitrary powers of arrest. They will be given a free hand in the development of surveillance and personal information systems. This will lead to an erosion of individual rights and it is quite conceivable that, in some democratic countries, the police or the army will take over government. This will be with the support of much of the population who will believe that a civilian democratic government cannot maintain law and order.

This may seem an alarmist scenario and it is admittedly an extreme extrapolation which we must hope never comes to pass. Nevertheless, it is short-sighted to ignore this possibility as an awareness of danger often allows that danger to be avoided. I personally believe that the erosion of democracy because of information technology will not be universal but will come about in some countries which are now democratic.

8.3.2 Automated utopia

The title of this section is, of course, frivolous as utopia is an unattainable ideal. Nevertheless, the title gets over the idea that the constructive use of information technology could result in a better quality of life for all and could lead to a more humane and just society.

We have already seen how technological unemployment could be eliminated by radical changes in our attitude to work and leisure. We have also seen that, in future, we need not be constrained to live in cities, to commute to work, or to undertake dreary, repetitive tasks. People could have more satisfying jobs, there could be less crime, less deprivation and less discrimination in our society. Rather than being treated as units of labour, people could do those tasks which cannot readily be automated and leave repetitive boring work to the machines.

Working from home, child rearing could be combined with work so that women could play a full and equal role in society. Information technology could be applied to all sorts of currently intractable problems so that energy and raw material utilisation is improved. In effect, we could use the power of computer and communication systems to determine how to make best use of natural resources, how to build very efficient machines which have minimal energy consumption, and how to reclaim waste material. This would mean less waste and pollution, and a slowing down of the exploitation of non-renewable natural resources. Solving these problems would create jobs and would improve the quality of life for everyone.

Although there would be a reduction in real disposable incomes, this need not necessarily mean a lower quality of life. Much of our incomes is spent replacing worn out products and buying energy which is used in a wasteful way. Our standard of living could be maintained simply by making better use of resources. Products could be built to last and planned obsolescence eliminated so that there would not be a constant need to replace objects. There could be more diversity in society where people had time to make things for themselves rather than buy mass-produced products. People could 'do their own thing' rather than be shackled to the treadmill of full-time employment. A country's or indeed the world's resources might be more evenly distributed so that extremes of poverty and affluence are eliminated.

Realistically, I do not think that this rosy view of a society without deprivation is very likely to come about in its entirety. However, aspects of such a society could become reality by the middle of next century if government, industry and the labour unions accept the challenges posed by information technology and react in an imaginative and innovative way. We are now at the threshold of a new age where information technology could lead to a better, more satisfying life for all.

Glossary

algorithm
> A precise statement of the steps involved in solving some problem. Examples of everyday algorithms are cooking recipes and assembly instructions. These can be termed 'informal algorithms' as they make lots of assumptions about the background knowledge of the reader. Algorithms intended to express a problem solution for a computer must be much more formal. They must logically set out each and every stage involved in going from an initial problem statement to a problem solution.

bandwidth
> A measure of the amount of information which can be transmitted along that cable. The bandwidth is determined by the material used in the cable, the cable construction, the environment in which the cable is laid, and the distance over which the information is to be transmitted. The amount of noise (q. v) limits the bandwidth of a cable.

bar code
> An identification code which is printed on product packaging. It consists of a sequence of black and white stripes of varying width with the stripe pattern identifying the manufacturer of the product and the product itself. Terminals equipped with bar code reading devices use the bar code to identify particular products.

BASIC
> A well known computer programming language. That is, it is a means of expressing algorithms (q.v.) in a form which can be understood and executed by a computer. BASIC is available on many if not all microcomputers (q.v.) and is best suited for writing fairly short computer programs. It is not suitable for writing computer programs which have more than a few hundred statements.

binary number

A sequence of 1s and 0s which expresses some numerical value. For example, in binary notation, the decimal number 27 is expressed as 11011. Binary numbers are the numbers used in systems where the base of the number system is 2. The derivation of binary numbers is analogous to the derivation of numbers in the more familiar decimal system where the system base is 10. For example, just as 327 means $3(100) + 2(10) + 7(1)$, 1011 in binary means $1(8) + 0(4) + 1(2) + 1(1)$.

computer-aided diagnosis

A system of medical diagnosis where the doctor makes use of a computer to help him arrive at a diagnosis. In its most common form, it involves programming a computer with the probability that particular symptoms are associated with particular conditions. The patient's symptoms are input to the computer and it responds with a list of possible conditions that the patient could be suffering from. Associated with each condition is a probability that the patient's symptoms are due to that condition.

computer-assisted learning (CAL)

An educational technique where a computer is used as an integral part of the educational process. The computer is programmed with educational material, a set of associated questions and the correct answers to these questions. The student is presented with the material then must answer the questions put by the computer. The machine compares the student's answers to the prepared answers and monitors his or her progress. As questions are correctly answered, the computer presents more and more advanced material. Incorrect answers cause the lesson taken by the student to be revised. Thus students can work individually, at their own pace, through the CAL lessons.

data base

A collection of information items grouped together and stored on a computer. In general, the grouping of the information is such that items can be readily retrieved by the computer user. Furthermore, existing items can be removed and new items added to the data base. Data bases usually contain large amounts of information. It is not unusual for such systems to hold information on millions of distinct entities such as people, products, etc.

182

data processing
A computer application which involves the processing of large amounts of commercial information. Typically, input data for a large number of items are prepared and then processed by the computer. The machine produces a corresponding set of output information. Data processing can be distinguished from other computer applications by the fact that all the input and output is in some standard format with identical operations carried out on each input item. Common data processing operations are stock control, the computing of sales invoices, and the calculation of payrolls.

debugging
The process of detecting and correcting errors in a computer program. These mistakes are usually made when a computer program is being written and result in the program producing incorrect output.

digital computer
An electronic device designed to manipulate binary numbers. The computer is made up of processing units which can identify and modify information and storage units which hold information either permanently or temporarily whilst it is being processed. Almost all computers nowadays are of this type as they are cheaper, more flexible and more accurate than other types of computational machinery. Digital computer is a generic term applied to all sizes of computer.

digitise
To convert some set of quantities to binary numbers of some form or another. For example, a line drawing can be digitised by considering it to be a rectangular array of binary digits (1s and 0s). Lines are represented by rows of 1s whereas white space is represented by zeros.

electronic funds transfer (EFT)
The direct transfer of funds from one bank account to another using computer and communication systems. No human intervention is required as the computers controlling financial transactions communicate directly to make that funds transfer.

electronic mail
A communications system which passes messages from one user of a computer to another via telecommunication lines. It has a number of advantages over conventional postal systems. The most important of these is the speed of transmission - messages can be delivered almost

instantly. In an electronic mail system, a central computer acts as a message sorter delivering messages addressed by the sender. There is no need for the sender to make a direct connection with the receiver of the message.

electronic point-of-sale (EPOS) terminal

A specialised type of computer terminal used in shops and stores. It combines the functions of a cash register and a computer terminal. As well as holding cash paid for goods and providing change, the EPOS terminal also includes a means of identifying the customer's purchases and transmitting that information to a central computer.

expert system

A computer system which is programmed with knowledge about some specialised topic. Expert systems include systems to diagnose some medical conditions, systems which understand the relationship of geological features and mineral deposits, and systems to diagnose faults in oil-rigs. The user of the system provides input information and the expert system integrates this with its own knowledge. It then comes to some conclusion which is presented to the user. The name expert system is used to denote the fact that the computer is really an expert in a particular field and that the knowledge built into the machine is comparable to that of a human expert.

fibre optic cable

A cable, made of glass rather than of copper, which is used in telecommunication systems. The information to be transmitted is represented as very short pulses of light, generated by a laser. Fibre optic cable has a very high bandwidth (q.v.) and is ideal for transmitting large amounts of computer data or television signals. A single fibre optic cable can carry hundreds of TV channels at the same time.

graphics tablet

A device which allows the user of a computer graphics system to mark positions on his or her screen or to draw pictures which can subsequently be 'remembered' by the computer. It is made up of a mesh of criss-crossing wires under a plastic surface cover. The user of the tablet 'draws' on it with a metal stylus. The position of this stylus on the tablet is detected by the computer and reflected on the screen. As the stylus is moved, the dot on the screen which represents the stylus position also moves.

heuristic

A heuristic process is a process of trial and error where solutions are generated and tested to see if they are satisfactory. A heuristic is some guide as to how the solutions can be generated so that those most likely to succeed are generated before other possible solutions.

information technology

A term embracing all those technologies which are involved in the creation, transmission, and processing of information. These include computer technology, television and video technology, and telecommunications technology. These previously diverse technologies are now converging and becoming interdependent so that, in future, a single information technology will come about.

local area network

A communications network which is restricted to some local area such as a suite of offices, a single floor of a building, or an assembly area in a factory. This network is usually set up as a ring of cable with devices plugged into the ring in the same way as electrical machinery can be plugged into a ring main. Because of their restricted size, local area networks allow very fast transmission of information from device to device.

mainframe computer

A somewhat arbitrary name applied to fast and powerful computers. The name is really related to the technology involved in building these machines and its derivation is too complicated to explain here. Essentially mainframe computers are both physically relatively large, have very large inbuilt memories and can process information very quickly indeed. They are used for such diverse applications as commercial data processing (q.v.), scientific calculations, and controlling a system of electronic point-of-sale (q.v.) terminals.

microchip

A chip of semiconductor material, usually silicon, which contains a single integrated circuit is termed a microchip. The chip varies in size from about 3mm square to about 12mm square, depending on the complexity of the circuit on the chip. The integrated circuit on the chip is formed from layers of silicon and metal film deposited on the chip.

microcomputer

A computer where the processing unit is contained

on a single microchip (q.v.). The essential
components are a microprocessor (q.v.) chip, a
number of microchips to act as a memory, a power
supply, and microchips which allow information to
be input and output.

microprocessor
A microchip where the circuit integrated onto the
chip is a computer processing unit - that is - the
part of a computer which can modify rather than
simply store information.

minicomputer
However, the term is usually applied to A computer
which is smaller and cheaper than a mainframe
computer and which does not have all of its
components integrated onto a single processor chip
like a microcomputer (q.v.). The term is somewhat
arbitrary - today's minicomputers are faster than
yesterday's mainframes.

noise
Spurious interference on a communication channel.
This interference is due to the environment of the
channel, the type of channel (broadcast, cable,
etc.), and the inherent physical characteristics of
the line material and construction.

packet
A group of binary digits which contains at least
the following information - the sender of the
packet, the receiver of the information and the
information being transmitted. Packets are usually
relatively short - hundreds of binary digits - and
it is usual to split a long message into many
distinct packets and transmit these individually.

PASCAL
A computer programming language available on many
microcomputers. It is better suited than
BASIC (q.v.) for writing large programs.

patient care system
A medical computing system which is used by medical
staff such as doctors or nurses to help them in
their work. Its function is to improve patient
care as opposed to many medical computing systems
which are designed to simplify and improve medical
administration.

pixel
An element of a picture generated by a computer.
Any picture can be considered to be made up of an
array of individual elements - for example, the

reproduction of a photograph in a newspaper is made up of many individual dots. When a picture is produced by a computer system each individual picture element is known as a pixel.

place notation

A mathematical term referring to the common notation which we use to represent numbers. The place of a digit in a number governs the actual quantity it represents. For example, in the number 777, the 7 in the rightmost place actual means the quantity 7, whereas the 7 in the leftmost place means the quantity 700. As we move from right to left, the digits represent increasing powers of the number system base.

plan detection

A technique used in artificial intelligence programs where the computer attempts to find out the intentions or plan of the user. The system has a built in set of possible intentions and the user's responses are analysed to see which of these inbuilt plans correspond most closely to his or her intention.

program

A set of instructions which a computer can carry out. It is usually written in some programming language like BASIC (q.v.) or PASCAL (q.v.) and then converted, by the computer itself, to binary numbers which can be interpreted by the machine. A program is a representation of an algorithm in a form which can be understood by a computer.

real-time computer system

A computer system which accepts information, processes it, them responds almost immediately in so-called 'real-time'. Typical real-time systems are process control systems which accept information from sensors then produce some output which modifies the process being carried out. For example, a temperature control system monitors the temperature and if it falls above or below a given level, causes a heater or a cooler to be switched on until the temperature is correct.

record

A collection of information about some single entity such as a person, a car, a book, a flight, etc. Data bases consist of many individual records, each associated with a single entity.

screen editor

A program which allows the user to modify

information displayed on his or her computer
terminal. The information to be changed is
modified simply by typing over the old information.
The computer detects which parts of the screen have
been overtyped and changes its internal
representation of the information accordingly.

script
A description of a set of actions which are typical
of some situation such as ordering a meal in a
restaurant, borrowing a book from a library, or
making a political speech. Scripts are used in
computer systems which are geared towards
understanding natural language. They allow
descriptions of situations to be placed in the
approriate context.

state indicator
An output device which reflects the current
condition of some other object. For example, a
thermometer on an office wall is a state indicator
giving the current state of the room temperature, a
counter on a tape recorder is a state indicator
giving information on the current state of the
tape.

teach and tell
A robot programming technique. An engineer makes
use of a manual control unit to guide the robot's
arm through the sequence of actions involved in
some process. The arm movements are recorded by
the robot's controlling computer and can then be
repeated automatically by the machine. This
technique is almost universally used for
programming the current generation of robots but in
future it is likely to be supplemented by other
techniques of control.

technological unemployment
Unemployment which results directly from the
introduction of new technology. For example, the
advent of the motor car caused technological
unemployment inasmuch as it made most of those
people concerned with looking after horses
redundant.

teleconferencing
A technique of computer communication where several
computer users in diverse locations can hold a
conference using their computer terminals for
communication. Some central machine acts as a
coordinator passing messages from participant to
participant. Teleconferencing is a specialised form
of electronic mail (q.v.).

teletext
A system which makes use of a conventional television screen to display textual information. In order to act as a teletext system, the TV must be converted to include a microprocessor and associated memory to control the storage and display of text.

ultra-intelligent machine
A hypothetical computer system whose intelligence surpasses human intelligence. As it is currently impossible to construct computer systems with even a fraction of the intellectual capabilities of humans, it is unlikely that such a machine will be built in the near future.

video disk
A plastic disk which can be used to record video information such as television pictures. These disks may also be used for storage of computer data and they offer opportunities to store very large amounts of data in a relatively small area. There are various video disk systems available with the most advanced system reliant on laser technology to read and store information on these disks.

videotex
A teletext system where the information displayed on the TV screen is transmitted to the TV via a communications line, normally that used by the telephone system. Users of videotex can call up individual pages for display on their screens. In this respect, videotex differs from broadcast teletext systems where information pages are generally broadcast to all users.

viewdata
Another (and, in my opinion, a more descriptive) name for videotex systems. However, there does now seem to be a standardisation on the term videotex to describe non-broadcast teletext systems.

Very Large Scale Integration (VLSI)
A technique for fabricating microchips where very large numbers of electronic components such as transistors are integrated onto a single chip of silicon.

voiceprint
An analysis of the sound patterns of an individual's voice. It seems that everyone has a unique voiceprint so it can be used as a means of identifying an individual in the same way as a fingerprint.

Reading list

In a book of this nature, it is not really appropriate to include a complete list of references to publications which I have used in preparing this text. Apart from the fact that many of these references are not written in an easily understandable way, they may not be readily available to many readers. In this section, therefore, I have listed some general reading on topics related to information technology. As a guide to the reader, I have also included some brief comments on each book listed below.

In a field such as information technology where new developments are happening all the time, it is inevitable that some of the material in these books is out of date. The best way to keep up with recent developments in the field is probably to read some of the increasing number of personal computing magazines which are now available. Although some of these are oriented towards providing listings of BASIC programs for computer games, the better ones provide details of new developments and are written in a clear and understandable way.

The following books may be of interest to the reader.

The Network Nation
Hiltz, S.R. & Turoff, M. 1978. Reading, Mass : Addison Wesley
Written by a computer scientist and a sociologist this book examines, in considerable detail, technical and social aspects of electronic mail and, particularly, computer conferencing. Although there is much of interest in this book, finding relevant material is difficult because the style of writing is rather verbose and the book has many, unnecessary verbatim quotes. Nevertheless, the book is probably essential reading for those who are seriously interested in how users react to electronic mail and conferencing systems.

The Mighty Micro
Evans, C. 1979. London : Victor Gollancz.
This book is a curious mixture of penetrating

insight and nonsense. It is written in a readable way, generally understandable by the non-technical reader. Evans clearly describes many novel applications of microelectronics but sometimes gets completely carried away in his extrapolation of trends. He tends to underestimate economic factors and the inertia of society in making his predictions of future microelectronic applications. Because some of his short-term predictions have manifestly failed to come true, his longer term predictions must also be treated with scepticism.

Future Developments in Telecommunications
Martin, J. 1977. Englewood Cliffs, New Jersey : Prentice-Hall.
This is an excellent introduction to telecommunications technology which can easily be understood by readers without a background in electronics. As Martin points out, the lead time from an invention to its widespread use is about 20 years so, in spite of the fact that this book was written in 1977, the material presented is still of relevance.

The Collapse of Work
Jenkins, C. & Sherman, B. 1979. London : Eyre Methuen
Written by prominent UK trade unionists, this book discusses the inevitability of technological unemployment and presents various suggestions of how to cope with the problem. The tone is realistic yet optimistic and the authors suggest that the problem can be tackled without radical social dislocations. The book has neither an index nor a reading list and this significantly reduces its usefulness.

Introducing the Electronic Office
Price, S.G. 1979. Manchester : NCC Publications.
This is a book which is written primarily for managers responsible for introducing automated office machinery. As well as discussing the scope and benefits of office automation, it also surveys current products and makes some predictions of future developments in this area.

Robots in Industry
Simons, G.L. 1980. Manchester . NCC Publications.
This is a reasonable survey of the existing state of the art of industrial robotics. Like 'Introducing the Electronic Office', it is written primarily for managers. The book covers the current state of robotics and its applications and it looks forward to potential developments in this field. Developments in this field have been very rapid since 1980 and the book is now slightly out of date.

Computer Power and Human Reason
Weizenbaum, J. 1976. San Francisco : Freeman
An anti-artificial intelligence polemic. Weizenbaum believes that it is morally wrong to try and imitate human intelligence by using a computer and he presents a convincing argument in this book. The book is now quite old and was written before artificial intelligence techniques had any commercial viability. Now that commercial applications of these techniques are in sight, I do not think that Weizenbaum's arguments will prevail.

The Conquest of Will
Mowshowitz, A. 1976. Reading, Mass : Addison Wesley
This is an excellent, well-written, book which ranges widely over the applications of computer systems and the effects of these systems on society. Mowshowitz also discusses the historical and cultural context of computing and considers how computers have been presented in literature. Although this book does not take into account recent developments in information technology, it is very worthwhile reading for anyone interested in computers and society.

Computers and the Cybernetic Society
Arbib, M. 1977. London : Academic Press
This book declares itself to be similar in scope to 'The Conquest of Will' discussed above but the author really concentrates more on introducing technical developments rather than discussing social implications at length. His technical descriptions are very good and unlike some introductory computing texts he doesn't get bogged down in details of computers. The sections of this book dealing with the simulation of complex systems and artificial intelligence are particularly good.

Artificial Intelligence
Winston, P. 1977. Reading, Mass : Addison Wesley
The first part of this book is quite a good introduction to artificial intelligence for the reader who has some programming experience and a knowledge of computing terminology. The second part, which introduces the LISP programming language is strictly for the professional or dedicated and advanced hobbyist who has access to a computer with this facility.

Information Technology
Zorkoczy, P. 1982. London : Pitman Books.
This is in introduction to information technology written by an electronics engineer. It concentrates mostly on the hardware - the authors background comes through very strongly - and the descriptions of the

electronic devices involved are very good. However, _
is very poor in its description of the applications of
information technology and on computer programming. It
says virtually nothing about the social implications of
this technology.

Microfuture
Shelley, J. 1981. London : Pitman
    This is a general introduction to computers with a
very definite orientation towards microprocessors. It
covers, in some detail, how computers work and how
microchips are made. It is, however, rather weak in
its   discussion   of   computer   applications   and
implications and its index is inadequate. However, for
the reader wishing to follow up some of the material in
Chapter 1 of this book, 'Microfuture' and 'Information
Technology' discussed above are reasonable starting
places.

The Making of the Micro
Evans, C. 1981. London : Gollancz
    This is a readable introduction to the history of
computers   covering   the   development   of   computing
machinery   from   the   abacus   to   the   microprocessor.
Sadly, the author died before the book was completely
finished and the later chapters, which deal with recent
developments, are a bit weak as they were completeted
by someone else. The style is chatty and, to my mind,
very irritating as it has many unnecessary asides.

Index